ITIL® Lifecycle Essentials

Your essential guide for the ITIL Foundation exam and beyond

ITIL® Lifecycle Essentials

Your essential guide for the ITIL Foundation exam and beyond

CLAIRE AGUTTER

IT Governance Publishing

IT Governance Publishing
IT Governance Limited
Unit 3, Clive Court
Bartholomew's Walk
Cambridgeshire Business Park
Ely
Cambridgeshire
CB7 4EA
United Kingdom

www.itgovernance.co.uk

© Claire Agutter 2013

First published in the United Kingdom in 2013
by IT Governance Publishing.

ISBN 978-1-84928-417-2

FOREWORD

It is so difficult when writing a good service management book to find the right level to pitch it. It can be hard to find a book that has simple enough language that it can accompany a student's foundation level studies, or act as an introduction to the topic. This book does that and provides, without question, a no nonsense interpretation of the key topics.

However, readers so often want much, much more. Claire Agutter has succeeded by adding a number of practical implementation tips drawn from her varied background and leveraging her experience. In short, Claire has managed to produce a publication you can use before, during and after ITIL® education, and dip into at any point during your IT service management improvement journey.

I feel certain you will enjoy reading Claire's publication and benefit from her insight, as you strive to influence the models you have used for implementing IT service management in your organisations.

So, what about the author? Claire commands a special place of notoriety in my career. Claire's unique position is as the only person I've ever interviewed for a service management lecturer / consultant role, who I have offered a job without seeing them, or asking them to do the obligatory 20-minute 'trial lecture' purgatory. Just 30 minutes of Claire's incredible passion for service management in a telephone interview was enough. Even then, for one so young, her knowledge, experience, enthusiasm and level-headed approach marked her out as one to watch in the role of future industry thought leader.

Careers develop and I went on to lead the best practice division at Global Knowledge, Chair itSMF UK and become Chief Examiner for ITIL Version 2 at APMG. Claire stayed in ITIL training, but moved away from the classroom forming her own company and producing some of the very best ITIL e-learning materials in the business. Claire's insight and down-to-earth approach are reflected in her book as much as they have in the assignments she has completed over the years.

Even though Claire's and my own career paths have separated, we still keep in touch and still share an undying passion for all things service management and giving back to the industry that has so enriched our careers. Claire has certainly 'given back' through this publication.

No matter where you are on your service management journey, may the fires of your passion for the topic burn brighter with every chapter. Happy reading.

Barry Corless

Business Development Director (Best Practice)

Global Knowledge

PREFACE

I've been involved with ITIL® and IT service management for more than 10 years. In that time, I've worked in operational and consulting roles, before moving into full-time ITIL training and certification. I've seen how happy customers are when IT works, and how angry they get when it doesn't.

Looking at the books available, it seemed to me there was little practical guidance for the new ITSM practitioner. There are the ITIL core volumes and lots of Foundation pass guides, but these don't add much value once your exam is complete.

This book contains everything you need to know to pass the ITIL Foundation Certificate in IT Service Management, but much more as well.

I've covered key processes and concepts that are not addressed as part of the Foundation syllabus, and provided some helpful, experience-based tips on using service management. For every process, I've added to the theory by including process considerations, based on my experience, and real-life service management, not just the ITIL core volumes.

As you progress through the book, you can easily see which content is related to the Foundation syllabus, and which isn't.

Content related to the Foundation syllabus is highlighted with this symbol:

Content that is not part of the Foundation syllabus is highlighted with this symbol:

I wish you every success in your ITIL Foundation exam, and hope you will continue to use this book as you work with IT service management in your day-to-day role.

Claire Agutter

Principal Lecturer

IT Training Zone Ltd.

ABOUT THE AUTHOR

Claire Agutter has been an ITIL principal lecturer since 2007. She has been involved in exam panels for ITIL V2 and V3, and provides online ITIL training through IT Training Zone Ltd.

Before working in ITIL training and education, she held a number of operational, consulting and implementation roles, giving her practical experience of ITIL in the real world.

After training hundreds of successful Foundation delegates, she has written this essential book to provide guidance for ITSM practitioners preparing for their Foundation exam and beyond.

ACKNOWLEDGEMENTS

We would like to acknowledge the following reviewers of this book for their useful contributions: Anna Leyland, Steria; Chris Evans, ITSM Specialist; Dave Jones, Pink Elephant; and John Custy, Managing Consultant, JPC Group.

CONTENTS

Contents

Contents

Contents

CHAPTER 1: INTRODUCING SERVICE MANAGEMENT

We're going to start this book by taking a look at what service management actually means. 'Service' and 'service management' are commonly used terms in the modern IT organisation, so it's worth spending some time analysing what they refer to and why they are important.

Why IT service management?

In today's world, information technology (IT) is a fully integrated part of everyone's life. Whether using a smartphone, withdrawing cash from an ATM, paying bills, or booking tickets on the Internet, IT is there in everything we do. It often plays a supporting role, so we don't even think about what we are using until it stops working.

In the modern business organisation, we see the same reliance on IT and IT services. Every department in the business, from finance and human resources through to logistics, relies on IT to carry out its role efficiently and effectively.

Effectiveness refers to whether IT is able to achieve its objectives. **Efficiency** refers to whether IT uses an appropriate amount of resources. An efficient IT service provider will use optimal amounts of time, money, staff, etc.

Now, more than ever, organisations need IT to survive. IT supports critical business processes that generate revenue, serve business customers and allow business goals to be achieved.

At the same time, the IT department or IT service provider is under more and more pressure to deliver better services, often at a reduced cost. There is a balance to find between supply and demand, service cost and service quality.

To make sure that IT can meet business objectives, organisations need service management. Service management makes sure that the IT services delivered do what the business needs, when the business needs it.

With effective support and good IT quality services, organisations can adopt bold strategies, including expansion of existing services and movement into new markets. With poor IT services, organisations will struggle to deliver what they do now, let alone expand and offer anything new or exciting.

In this chapter, we're going to take a look at some of the key concepts related to service management. Every IT organisation that wants to survive must understand and embrace these concepts.

Service

The dictionary definition of a service is related to helping someone. To do someone a service means that you have offered help or assistance.

This maps easily onto the IT services we use every day. Services should make our lives easier – if they don't, there is no reason to use them, or spend money providing and maintaining them.

You can see the ITIL definitions for a service and an IT service in Table 1, below:

Service	*'A service is a means of delivering value to customers by facilitating outcomes customers want to achieve without the ownership of specific costs and risks.'*
IT service	*'A service provided by an IT service provider. An IT service is made up of a combination of information technology, people and processes. A customer-facing IT service directly supports the business processes of one or more customers, and its service level targets should be defined in a Service Level Agreement. Other IT services, called supporting services, are not directly used by the business, but are required by the service provider to deliver customer-facing services.'*

Table 1: Service definitions

ITIL recommends the development of **outcome-based** definitions of services. This means that we need to look at the customer outcome that the service delivers, not the technology the IT service provider is offering to the customer.

For example, a customer may pay to have access to a cloud-based hosting service for their company website. The service provider might think of the service in terms of server space, back-up schedules, connectivity and power management. The customer thinks of the service in terms of their website being available and accessible to customers who are buying from them. These are the outcomes that matter.

An outcome is: *'the result of carrying out an activity, following a process or delivering an IT service. Outcome can refer to intended or actual results.'*

Not all IT services work as hoped when they first go live, but we need to be able to quantify the outcome they were supposed to deliver to assess whether it's worth keeping the service.

Customers need to trust their service provider, and believe that the service will continue to meet their needs in the future. If they don't trust the service provider, the relationship between customer and service provider will probably be quite brief.

Customer expectations will not stay the same. They will change over time. Service providers must track and understand their customer's expectations and update services to make sure they are still delivering value.

It is very important for a service provider to understand the services they are offering and what they mean to customers. This includes looking at how services relate to each other, and which customers use which services.

If a service is performing poorly and doesn't have many customers, it may be retired. A service that is performing well and attracting many customers may receive more investment.

Service classification

Services can be broken down into classifications to make them easier to understand and manage. You can see the three main service classifications in Table 2, overleaf:

Core services	*'Core services deliver the basic outcomes desired by one or more customers. These services represent the value the customer wants and will pay for.'* These attract the customer in the first place. Customers must be satisfied with the core services. E-mail, for example, could be a core service that allows the customer to access messaging functionality.
Enabling services	*'Enabling services need to be in place for the core service to be delivered.'* The customer may not even know the enabling service exists, but it is essential. Customers will not see enabling services as being services that they use. They are basic factors that make sure the core services can be delivered. The network might be an enabling service for the e-mail service offered to customers. It must be in place and working for e-mail to be accessible.
Enhancing services	Enhancing services are non-essential services that are added to the core service to tempt or excite the customer. There is always a danger that customers will get used to having access to enhancing services, and see them as being part of the core service. Service providers need to make sure they review their enhancing services regularly and update them if necessary. The e-mail service might be enhanced by offering calendar functionality, or mobile e-mail.

Table 2: Service classifications

Service packages

Service providers can use service packages to help them offer their services to customers in a more attractive and meaningful way. Service packages are made up of combinations of core, enabling and enhancing services. The package contains two or more services that have been bundled together to meet the customer's needs. For example, when you enter into a mobile phone contract, you might be offered a special rate for international calls, if you are a frequent traveller. The core service can have different options added to it to make it more attractive to you, the customer.

Customers will want different levels of service as part of their service package. These different levels are documented in a Service Level Package, which is then delivered with the service package. The Service Level Package allows customers to choose service targets that are appropriate for their needs. For example, they might choose a bronze, silver or gold service with different service hours and support options.

Creating a service package with just the right combination of services and service levels will make sure that customers are kept happy. They will be able to pay for what they want, and shouldn't be forced to pay for any extras they don't want access to.

 ## Internal and external services

Internal services are delivered to departments or business units in the same organisation as the service provider. For example, the internal IT department might be delivering services to the finance and human resources department in the same organisation.

External services are delivered to an external customer, who could be an individual, or another organisation. You might be an external customer for your internet service provider at home. The organisation you work for might buy all, or part, of its IT services from third-party external providers.

Internal services usually support internal activity. For example, human resources might use an internal IT service to manage payroll and track expenditure on employee training.

External services usually support business outcomes. If an organisation sells products via a website, the external services are the website, online stock system and so on.

It's usually easier to see how external services create value. For example, if our website is unavailable, we can't take any orders and lose £10,000 an hour. This is a tangible and quantifiable result. We might also suffer reputation damage. This is harder to quantify, but still relevant.

Internal services would need to be linked to external services for their value to be understood. For example, if the rota system is unavailable staff will not arrive at work when they should, meaning orders can't be fulfilled and we lose £10,000 an hour.

For public sector or non-profit organisations, the value of a service needs to be assessed against other meaningful outcomes, such as domestic waste not being collected, or hospital appointments not being made.

In the public sector the risk associated with a service being unavailable can be very different to that of the private sector. Private sector organisations often think in terms of profit or loss; the public sector might think about the impact on people's lives.

 Types of service

There are also different types of service, as illustrated in Table 3.

Supporting service	Supporting services are often infrastructure services. They need to be in place for other services to be delivered, but the business might not be aware of them. For example, the network is a supporting service. If the network isn't available, many other services will be unavailable.
Internal customer facing services	These are used by customers in the same organisation as the service provider. For example, a finance team might use an accounting service to track payments that have been made.
External customer facing services	Here, the customer is not part of the same organisation as the service provider. For example, when you use an ATM you are an external customer for that particular service.

Table 3: Service types

📋 Service management

Services deliver **value** to customers. They can't work properly if they aren't carefully managed. An IT service needs to be measured, monitored and maintained in order to continue working effectively. An IT service provider can't just put a service into the live environment and forget about it.

ITIL is described as best practice for the management of IT services. It doesn't matter what job you have in IT, your role is part of the overall service that is being offered to the customer.

Most modern organisations rely on IT to be effective. They expect IT to be available, responsive and communicate with them regularly. Technology alone does not deliver a good service. Technology needs to be managed in order to meet the customer's needs.

The definition of service management is *'a set of specialized organizational capabilities for providing value to customers in the form of services'.*

Capabilities refer to how good an organisation is at carrying out a task or activity. The more mature the organisation, the better its capabilities should be. Capabilities will be based on an organisation's experience of customers, processes, services, tools, market conditions, etc. This experience grows over time.

Organisations develop service management capabilities and skills so they can respond to challenges. There are four specific challenges that shape an organisation's service management capabilities. These challenges are:

- the intangible nature of the output of a service process

- demand for services is tightly coupled to the customer's assets
- the high level of contact between the service provider and the customer, or service consumer
- the perishable nature of service output and capacity.

Table 4, below, considers these challenges in more detail.

The intangible nature of the output of a service process	Examples of services could include application hosting, or data storage. These can be difficult to measure and control. Many service providers have thought they were delivering a good service, only to have a customer complain about something like 'slow performance'.
Demand for services is tightly coupled to the customer's assets	Services are not tangible outputs, such as cars or televisions. They cannot be stockpiled if too many are produced. Service providers need to be able to respond to increases in customer demand, without having too much unused capacity. Documents such as contracts and Service Level Agreements can help to address this challenge by defining, agreeing, documenting and reviewing customer requirements.
The high level of contact between the service provider and the customer or service consumer	Often, the customer and supplier of a service are part of the same organisation. Defining and managing the roles, interfaces and overlaps between them can be extremely difficult. Many service providers adopt formal service management frameworks, like ITIL, to provide structure and replace informal agreements based on personal networks and relationships.

The perishable nature of service output and capacity	Customers need assurance that service will continue to be delivered to the required level of quality.
	The service provider needs to be assured of ongoing customer demand before they will invest in services and infrastructure.
	An ongoing relationship will provide certainty that will benefit the customer and the service provider.

Table 4: Service management challenges

 Service management as a professional practice

Service management should be viewed as a professional practice. It is supported by an extensive body of knowledge, experience and skills that have built up as the IT industry matured and developed a service focus.

There is a global community of professionals that support service management, including organisations like the IT Service Management Forum. You can read more about the itSMF at *www.itsmfi.org*, including finding out about your national chapter and any resources that are available to support you. The itSMF allows service management practitioners to connect with each other and share feedback and experience.

Service management is also supported by a scheme that provides quality assured education, training and certification.

There is a wealth of service management information available – including academic research and formal standards related to services and service management, such as ISO/IEC 20000.

Service management has developed as IT's focus has moved from a technology-centric approach to an end-to-end service approach. The new approach focuses on the customer and the quality of service they receive. IT is increasingly seen as a vital business enabler, and IT plans must be aligned to overall business models, strategies and plans.

Another factor that has contributed to the advancement and development of service management is the increasing complexity of service delivery. More and more organisations are using shared services, or have outsourced some or all of IT to external service providers. As more and more stakeholders form part of service delivery, more and more sophisticated service management is required to control it. As supply chains get more complex, the service management processes that control them need to get better and better. The increased complexity of delivery has strengthened and improved service management, as well as imposing greater challenges on it.

IT service management

IT organisations need to work hard to understand what their customers need from them. They are a service provider to their customer, using service management to deliver the customer's desired outcomes. IT service management needs to be efficient and effective, delivering high quality IT services.

IT service providers usually have to balance three areas:

- what the customer wants
- how the service performs
- how much the customer is willing to pay.

If IT can't deliver what the customer wants at the right price, they need to communicate this as soon as possible. Documents such as Service Level Agreements can be used to help manage expectations and make sure the customer and service provider have a clear understanding of what is meant to be delivered for each service.

Stakeholders

If IT doesn't understand what the business wants, it has no hope of being able to deliver services to meet business needs. The IT service provider needs to build relationships with stakeholders to improve communication and really get to know its customers. A stakeholder is defined as *'any person who has an interest in an organisation, project, IT service or other area. Stakeholders may be interested in activities, targets, resources or deliverables.'*

Stakeholders can be anyone – internal or external to the organisation. Service providers will often deal with three main groups:

- **Customers:** *'customers buy goods or services'*. They will define what the service does, but may not use it regularly.
- **Users:** use the service bought by the customer on a regular basis.
- **Suppliers:** third parties who are involved in part or all of the service delivery.

Customers

The customers who decide what services are needed are often IT's most important stakeholders. They shape the services that IT delivers and make funds available for the provision of services.

IT needs to develop a close relationship with its customers. This will often involve understanding the business processes that they use and the roles that they fulfil. Some IT organisations say 'our customers don't understand what we do – why do we need to understand what they do?' This is a dangerous position. An IT organisation that understands its customer can make positive suggestions and support them. They will be seen as valuable, and the customer/IT service provider relationship will be strong.

Internal customers

Internal customers are part of the same organisation as the service provider. For example, the human resources department might commission a service to track employee-training records.

The IT service provider will share the same business objectives as internal customers. They can be easier to talk to, as they are part of the same organisation, but IT may find it has to balance the conflicting needs of different internal customers.

Internal customers can also be challenging, because the relationship with them is often informal. Joe Bloggs that you have lunch with in the canteen every day might also be your customer, and expect more based on your friendship.

Internal customers might receive services that are centrally funded as part of the organisation's budgeting cycle. If an IT service provider receives funding to support multiple internal customers, it can be difficult to decide where to invest and what projects should be given priority.

 ## *External customers*

External customers are not part of the same organisation as the service provider and will be paying directly for goods and services. The relationship will probably be on a more formal level, backed up by contractual agreements.

External customers may be easier to work with because the nature of the relationship has been clearly defined from the start. However, if the customer has not explained what they need, or the service provider has agreed to a service they don't have the capabilities to deliver, the relationship will deteriorate quickly.

External customers may feel that they are paying the bills, so they get to tell the service provider how it's going to be.

 ## Types of service provider

We've already used the term 'service provider' many times in this volume. There are three main types of service provider. They will share some goals (such as keeping their customers happy), but also have some crucial differences.

 ## *Type 1 Service Providers*

Type 1 Service Providers are also referred to as internal service providers. They are typically embedded within the

business unit they serve, and will provide business functions such as finance, logistics, IT and human resources. Type 1 Service Providers do not have a great degree of autonomy and cannot set their own policies. They operate strictly within the requirements of the business unit – which often funds them through overheads. This close relationship delivers one of the main benefits of a Type 1 Service Provider. They are very closely linked to their customers, and their customer's required outcomes, which removes some of the risks associated with working with an external supplier.

The strategic direction of the Type 1 provider is normally set by the managers of the business unit they are serving. It will be the business unit that defines the services on offer, the level of investment and the metrics to be reported against.

Because of the limited customer base of the Type 1 Service Provider, they are typically at greater risk of market failure, as they are affected by peaks and troughs of demand. They can be compared unfavourably to competitors from outside the business unit, who serve more than one customer, have more autonomy and can provide economies of scale.

Another issue associated with Type 1 Service Providers is the possibility of duplication and greater cost when a number of Type 1 providers are maintained within one organisation.

 Type 2 Service Provider

Type 2 Service Providers are also known as the shared services unit. They offer services to all business units in the

organisation, rather than being embedded within one business unit, or department.

This type of service provider has much more autonomy, and their direction is not necessarily set by the individual business unit managers. The shared services unit treats all business units as customers, and behaves more like an external service provider. It will tailor its services to attract, satisfy and maintain its customer base.

The Type 2 Service Provider is vulnerable to being compared with external service providers and may be at risk of outsourcing, or substitution, if they are not competitive. They need to be able to demonstrate advantages from the continuation of the shared services unit.

The customers of a shared services unit are business units within a common corporate parent. Some business units may receive a poorer service from the shared services unit than they would from a Type 1 provider, but this will be balanced out by gains at the corporate level.

Any decisions about moving to a Type 2 provider will need to be made at a senior management or corporate level, or the shared services unit will not be accepted.

 Type 3 Service Provider

Type 3 Service Providers are external service providers. They specialise in the delivery of a particular type of service, and may be able to offer competitive prices, expertise and best practice unavailable to the customer internally.

Often, the core business of a Type 3 Service Provider is service provision. They can excel in this, unlike the service consumer who may see management of an area like the Service Desk as an unwelcome administrative headache.

External suppliers may also be chosen when the business strategy is looking to reduce fixed costs and operational risks, or is looking to become more lean and flexible. Buying a service may suit the strategic direction better than operating the service in house. Type 3 Service Providers, due to their breadth and depth of service, may also be able to provide elements that a Type 2 or Type 1 Service Provider would be unable to offer.

There are risks associated with Type 3 Service Providers. These include, choosing a service provider with different goals or priorities that do not align with the purchasing organisation; security risks where multiple customers from the same industry are served; and also the risk of a Type 3 Service Provider ceasing to trade. Internal capabilities for the customer may also be reduced, as they are no longer building up knowledge in house.

The customer organisation will have to make a balanced decision based on benefits, such as cost savings, weighed against risks, such as the loss of internal knowledge.

ITIL and the service provider types

The guidance available in the ITIL framework is relevant for all service provider types. Each type of service provider will have different goals and may need to tailor the ITIL processes to help meet these, but this doesn't mean ITIL is irrelevant.

There is still a common perception that ITIL is only suitable for certain sectors or sizes of organisation – this is not the case. Every IT service provider, for example, needs a Change Management process. The type and size of the service provider will influence how that process is implemented, but does not affect the underlying reason for having a process.

🗎 Why ITIL?

So, with all this in mind, we need to ask 'what is ITIL and why is it important?' ITIL is considered to be best practice for IT service management. It was developed by the UK Government, and is now globally adopted by many organisations in both the public and private sector.

ITIL is not a prescriptive standard that must be followed. It does not say what must be done in a service provider organisation, and there is no certificate or award for successfully adopting ITIL. Instead, ITIL is a **framework** that organisations can adopt and adapt to improve the way they deliver their IT services.

ITIL is a widely recognised source of best practice. It supports organisations as they deliver services that meet their customer's needs, at a price their customer is willing to pay.

In today's climate, organisations cannot afford to stand still. They need to review their performance and compare it to their competitors, and make sure they are constantly improving. Using the best practice available in the public domain can support internal improvement. Sources, including public frameworks like ITIL and standards such as ISO/IEC 20000, can all be used to add value.

ISO/IEC 20000 is the standard for service management, and is used to certify an organisation's processes and management systems. If organisations benchmark themselves against their competitors and continue to invest in skills and capabilities, they will remain competitive.

This thinking does not just apply to the private sector. Public sector organisations, such as local and central government departments also need to demonstrate that they offer quality services and value for money. They might not be measured on profit, but there will be service objectives that they have to meet.

 Why ITIL has been successful

ITIL is not academic and theoretical. It is based on the experience of IT service management practitioners, and offers a practical, process-led approach that has evolved over many years. The introduction of a service focus means that IT stops thinking about technology, and starts to think about how to deliver value to the customer.

Common processes and practices and a strong service management framework all help to support the focus on value.

ITIL is successful because:

- **It's vendor neutral:** ITIL is not linked to one supplier, or one technology, or one industry. This means it can be adopted across all types and sizes of organisation.
- **It's non-prescriptive:** Organisations need to adopt and adapt the elements of ITIL that work for them and their customers.

- **It's best practice:** ITIL draws on experience from service management practitioners across the globe.

Best practice simply means *'proven activities or processes that have been successfully used in multiple organisations'*.

ITIL is seen as being preferable to the proprietary knowledge that builds up in organisations and staff members. Proprietary knowledge isn't usually documented in a consistent way. It exists because it has built up over time. This means it is not challenged or improved – and can cause a real risk if an experienced staff member leaves and takes their proprietary knowledge with them.

Figure 1, overleaf, shows the many sources of service management practice. Any practices that an organisation is going to adopt must be passed through a filter of the drivers and scenarios relevant to the organisation, before it is fit for purpose. For example, a financial organisation cannot just pick up the ITIL books and implement ITIL immediately. They need to assess what regulations they have to comply with, what their competitors are doing, and what their customers want before they can go ahead.

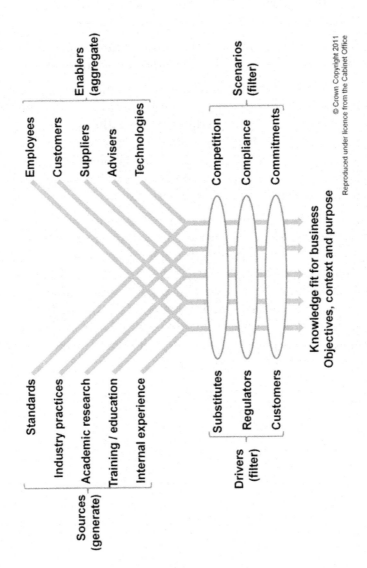

Figure 1: Service management practice

CHAPTER 2: KEY CONCEPTS AND ROLES

Most organisations recognise that they need some form of IT service management. Actually putting something in place to meet that need can be much more challenging. In this chapter, we're going to study some of the key components of a service management capability: processes, functions and generic roles.

 Processes

The ITIL definition of a process is:

'A process is a structured set of activities designed to accomplish a specific objective. A process takes one or more defined inputs and turns them into defined outputs.'

To be effective, service management processes should be set up as closed-loop systems. This means that they request feedback, and use that feedback to improve the way they perform. If processes don't work on this closed-loop model, they will not improve and no lessons will be learned.

Processes should also be documented, so they can be shared and used throughout an organisation. If there isn't a definitive agreed version of a process, different teams will carry out the activities in different ways – all of them believing they are following the process properly.

Processes are directed by policies. Policies are used to document management expectations and their intentions for the process. The policy is then used to make sure the process development and implementation is done in a way that is consistent with management intentions.

Within service management, one of the ways that processes deliver value is by being reusable. This means, for example, that one Change Management process can be used across the organisation, rather than each programme or project developing its own Change Management process. Reusable processes can be measured, monitored and improved.

 Process model

To support organisational understanding of processes, we can document them using a process model. A process model is a way of designing and mapping a process, and can be very effective if you need to develop a brand new process, or update an existing one. Figure 2, overleaf, shows a process model.

Every process has to have inputs and outputs. An input triggers a process, for example, a call to a Service Desk will start the fault resolution or diagnostic process.

Outputs mean the iteration of the process is complete and it has served its purpose. As part of the output, we ask for feedback, which makes sure our process is working as a closed loop – learning lessons about how it is working and the level of customer satisfaction.

Activities that need to happen to turn the input into an output are documented in the 'process' box. These activities include roles, procedures, workflows and metrics.

Process controls are in place to make sure the process works properly and doesn't become ineffective over time. Controls include the process owner, the policy and the feedback that we receive.

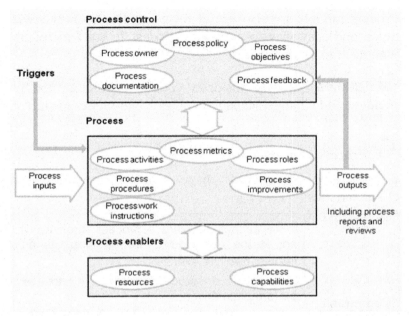

Figure 2: The process model

Process enablers are the resources that we use to make the process work, for example, technology or people. A perfect process will deliver no value if there aren't enough resources to implement it.

Remember: a process model doesn't have to be complicated. You can start by brainstorming the process with a group of stakeholders. This will help you to get the right steps documented, so that they can be agreed. Once a common process is defined and agreed, you can automate it using a service management toolset, if appropriate.

Process models are also useful for education, as they are a quick and easy way to explain a process to staff members who need to learn about it.

 Have a go: why not draw your own process model? Incident and Change Management are great places to start.

Process characteristics

Every process should have the following four characteristics:

Measurable	If we cannot measure a process, then it will not fit the definition of closed loop, as no feedback will be available. Measuring a process allows it to be performance driven. Different measurements will be required for different audiences, for example, managers may be interested in the cost of the process, while customers may be interested in the outcome.
Delivers specific results	The results of a process need to be identifiable, measureable and countable. Again, without a clear result the process cannot be managed, measured and controlled. If a process does not have a defined result, or end-point, it could in theory go on forever.
Delivers to a customer or stakeholder	The customer or stakeholder can be internal or external, but it is their expectations that shape the overall process.

Responds to specific triggers	The trigger or input to the process is important for measurement and control. Unless we understand when the process starts, we won't know what point to measure from.

Table 5: Process characteristics

 Functions

'A function is a team or group of people and the tools or other resources they use to carry out one or more processes or activities.'

Functions are used to structure organisations. The individual resources that make up a function need to communicate well with each other and with other functions. A key part of service management is making sure that functions interact effectively. The Service Desk and second-line support are common IT functions. If the Service Desk has a very poor relationship with second-line support, this might mean that incidents aren't resolved as quickly as they should be.

If functions are not working as well as they should, senior management may look to restructure the organisation into a different functional structure. They might also introduce processes that link functions together, to show the teams how they should be working.

Functions are used across the service lifecycle, for example, there may be a Change Management function responsible for the Change Management process, or a Service Level Management function responsible for agreeing and maintaining Service Level Agreements.

In this book, we'll only consider the Service Operation functions in detail. ITIL cannot dictate how an organisation should be structured, and each service provider organisation will develop its own ideal structure over time.

Roles

'A role is a set of responsibilities, activities and authorities granted to a person or team. A role is defined in a process or function. One person or team can have multiple roles.'

Roles are carried out by people, and need to be clearly outlined so that people understand what they are supposed to do. Clear roles and responsibilities are essential for an effective service management organisation. If roles are not clear, tasks may be duplicated – or not done at all.

Remember: a single person can fulfil many roles – that's why it is so important to map roles carefully.

Many organisations that are new to ITIL and service management look at all of the ITIL processes and panic. They think they need to hire hundreds of new staff to fulfil all of the roles – confusing a job or person and a role.

In a smaller organisation, one person may have lots of roles. ITIL doesn't mean hiring lots of staff, it simply means matching up the service management roles with the existing IT staff members. For example, one staff member might carry out Change Management and Configuration Management roles. Service Desk staff might have roles within the Incident Management, Access Management and Request Fulfilment processes.

📋 *The RACI model*

RACI models are used to manage resources and roles for the delivery of a piece of work or task. Resources can be drawn from different functional areas, which makes it challenging for line managers to track what their staff are doing. For example, a technical resource might be involved with incident investigation, problem resolution, a project and working with a new supplier.

The RACI model is used to track who is doing what. It provides clear mapping of roles across the different teams in the organisational structure. RACI stands for Responsible, Accountable, Consulted and Informed.

Only one person can be **Accountable** for any task. The person who is accountable for the task has the overall authority for the task – but they may not carry out individual pieces of work themselves.

Any number of people can be **Responsible** as part of the RACI model. These are the workers who will get the actual tasks done, and they will report to the **Accountable** resource about their progress.

Sometimes resources are **Consulted** to get a task done. This might be a person within the organisation who has specific knowledge, or it could be a document store, or even an internet search engine. These resources need to be tracked to ensure they are available when required.

Other resources need to be **Informed**. These resources are stakeholders who need to track and understand exactly how the task is progressing, or they may need an output from the task. Business sponsors, for example, will typically be informed about progress as part of a project.

When RACI is applied to service management processes, the process owner will be accountable for all the process activities, even if they are not responsible for carrying them out.

RACI models are often shown as a matrix. To build a RACI matrix, these steps need to be followed:

- identify activities
- identify roles
- assign RACI codes
- identify gaps or overlaps
- distribute the chart for feedback
- monitor the roles.

Have a go: why not draw your own RACI matrix? You will also find many examples on the Internet. Table 6, below, shows an example of a RACI matrix for a coffee shop making a customer's coffee order.

Fulfilling a coffee order	Customer	Store owner	Staff member	Supplier
Providing staff		A	R/C	
Providing premises		A	R	
Providing ingredients		A	C	R
Providing order details	A/C		R/I	
Making coffee	C/I		A/R	
Confirmation of order fulfilment	I		A/R	
Drinking and approving coffee	A/R	I	I	

Table 6: Simple RACI matrix

Generic service management roles

Every organisation is different, so service management guidance can't provide an organisation chart that will work for everyone. There are, however, some generic service management roles that need to be assigned to make sure that services and processes are looked after properly.

Remember: these are roles, not people.

 Process owner

A process owner is responsible for ensuring that a process is both fit for purpose and performing adequately. The process owner's accountabilities include:

- defining the process strategy
- assisting with process design, including the design of process metrics
- making sure the process is documented
- auditing the process
- addressing any issues or opportunities for process improvement
- defining policies and standards related to the process
- sponsoring the process.

The process owner role should be assigned to a single person – it should not be shared. A team, for example, should not be allocated ownership of a process – it has to be a single person or role. This allows the process owner to manage the process effectively with no duplication or confusion.

Process manager

The process manager is accountable for the operational management of a process. There can be more than one manager for each process, for example, an organisation might have regional change managers, each providing process management for their area.

In a small organisation, the process manager and owner might be the same person. In a larger organisation, they may be separate. This will be an organisational decision based on the size of the organisation and the number of staff available, as well as the complexity of the process.

The process manager's accountabilities include:

- working with the process owner
- making sure all process activities are carried out
- appointing staff to process roles and managing resources
- monitoring and reporting on process performance
- working with service owners and other process managers to make sure processes support services
- identifying improvements and working with the Continual Service Improvement manager to prioritise them
- making improvements to process implementation.

 Process practitioner

This role actually carries out the process activities. In smaller organisations, this role may be combined with the process manager. In larger organisations there may be multiple practitioners for each process. Again, this will be an organisational decision dictated by the context in which the process operates. Examples of process practitioners could include incident analysts, change management analysts, service level reporting staff, etc.

The process practitioner will be responsible for the following areas:

- carrying out process activities
- understanding how their role links to services and creates value
- working with other stakeholders involved with the process
- making sure that inputs, outputs and interfaces are correct
- creating or updating records of their activities.

 Service owner

The service owner is accountable for the delivery of a specific IT service. As with the process owner, the service owner may not carry out all the activities involved in service delivery, but they do need to make sure that all of the work is carried out and the service is delivered as agreed.

The service owner is responsible to the customer for the initiation, transition and ongoing maintenance and support of the service. They are also accountable to the IT director for service delivery. The role is responsible for continual improvement of their service and management of any changes associated with it. In a smaller organisation, one person may fulfil the service owner role for many services.

Other responsibilities for the service owner include:

- attending the Change Advisory Board to assess the impact of changes to their service
- attending internal and external service review meetings
- communicating with customers about service-related enquiries and issues
- serving as a point of escalation (including for major incidents)
- participating in Service Level Agreement and Operational Level Agreement negotiations.

To make sure their service is working as it should, they will interface with many service management processes, including Business Relationship Management.

⊟ CHAPTER 3: THE SERVICE LIFECYCLE

ITIL is based around a service lifecycle with five phases, which has been documented as five core volumes. These cover a service's life from start to finish, from conception through to ongoing improvement. These five volumes are referred to as the **core** of ITIL, and they provide high-level guidance and process information across the complete service lifecycle. The volumes are:

- *Service Strategy*
- *Service Design*
- *Service Transition*
- *Service Operation*
- *Continual Service Improvement.*

The core is also supplemented by another series of books known as **complementary guidance**. The complementary publications provide further guidance that is more specific to industry sectors, organisation types, operating models, and technology architectures. As ITIL becomes more widely adopted and matures further, the amount of complementary guidance available will increase.

The service lifecycle diagram (*see Figure 3*) is a visual representation of how the five phases fit together.

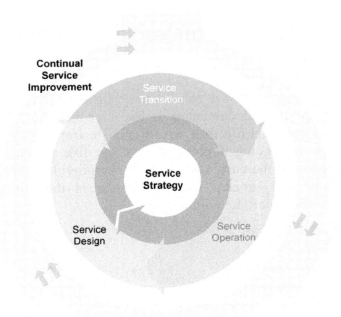

Figure 3: The service lifecycle

Service Strategy is the hub that drives the lifecycle. Continual Service Improvement looks for improvement opportunities in all stages. Service Design, Transition and Operation work together as a network.

We will review the stages of the lifecycle at a high level in this chapter, before we look at each stage in more detail later in this publication.

When we study the individual stages of the lifecycle in detail, we discuss the processes that are relevant for that stage. Each process is described in the lifecycle stage where it carries out its most critical role. For example, Availability Management is discussed in Service Design, because it is so important to design availability into new or changed services. If availability isn't designed into services, it will have to be retro-fitted after they have gone live. This is much more expensive and disruptive for end users.

However, this doesn't mean that processes stop working once their lifecycle stage is complete. Many processes have an ongoing role throughout the service lifecycle, for example, Availability Management will be active in Service Transition and Service Operation, and will work with Continual Service Improvement. Bear this in mind as we review the service management processes.

 Service Strategy

 Purpose and objectives

Service Strategy is the centre of the lifecycle and the hub that all the other phases revolve around. The purpose of Service Strategy is to define what a service provider needs to do in terms of service delivery to support its customer(s). The strategy that is adopted must support the customer's desired business outcomes.

As part of its purpose, Service Strategy will define plans, patterns, a position and perspective for how the service provider will behave. These are used to help cascade the strategy down through the organisation, and make sure that all parts of IT behave consistently.

Service Strategy has a number of objectives. These objectives will help to define how the rest of the service lifecycle works.

Although many of the staff working in an IT organisation will not actually get involved in making strategic decisions, they will be affected by them. If the decisions are wrong – or not thought through correctly – they can have a negative effect on all areas of the organisation. For example, strategic decisions might be made that reduce staff levels in the IT organisation. This will affect people working at the operational level who may find they are expected to do more, or are put under more pressure.

The Service Strategy objectives include:

- understanding what strategy is
- understanding what services are, and who the organisation's customers are
- understanding how value is created and delivered
- creating a service provision model to show how services will be delivered and funded
- understanding if the service provider organisation is capable of delivering the strategy, and what needs to be done if it isn't
- identifying opportunities to offer services and being able to act on them
- understanding what service assets make up services and managing them appropriately
- putting processes in place to make sure the strategy is delivered.

 Scope

The scope of Service Strategy includes defining principles and processes for service management, which then apply to the rest of the service lifecycle. Internal and external IT service providers both need a coherent strategy to make sure their services deliver value.

The scope of Service Strategy can be broken down into two areas:

- defining a strategy for how the service provider will deliver services that meet customer needs
- defining a strategy for ongoing management of services.

 Value

A well-thought-out strategy will provide many benefits for an organisation. Effective Service Strategy helps organisations to:

- offer appropriate services that meet business needs
- offer the services in a timely way
- link IT activities and assets to business outcomes to show the true value of IT
- demonstrate return on IT investment and value for money
- be seen as a trusted partner by customers.

 **Service Design**

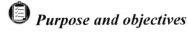 *Purpose and objectives*

Once a strategy has been defined and communicated, services can be designed to meet the strategic objectives. The purpose of the Service Design stage of the lifecycle is to design services that fulfil the strategic objectives, which are based on business requirements.

IT processes, practices and policies also need to be designed to make sure that services are high quality, cost effective, and meet customer needs.

The main objective of Service Design is to deliver a service which works. This means that the service won't need significant improvement when it is live, ultimately reducing the cost of delivering the service. All Service Design activities must have continual improvement embedded in them, so that solutions and designs are always getting better.

 Scope

The scope of Service Design includes the design of appropriate and innovative services that meet business needs – now and in the future. There are a number of Service Design processes and concepts that support this, which we'll look at in later chapters.

Service Design will be influenced by requirements, business benefits and constraints. If the business has set a budget for a service, Service Design has to make sure it stays within that budget.

 Value

You may already understand the value of good Service Design practices, based on your own experience. You might have received a new service that didn't work as it should, or you might have had to support a service that didn't meet customer expectations.

Service Design helps organisations to:

- improve service quality, so that services meet business needs from the start
- make sure services are implemented well and consistently
- make sure services perform in line with agreed business requirements
- reduce service costs, including the cost of redesign and rework
- improve governance and decision making
- improve service management and process design.

 Service Transition

Once a service has been designed, it will be transitioned into the live environment.

Service transitions need to be carefully planned and managed, as they have the potential to negatively affect live services. A transition might fail, meaning a new service is not accessible. That will be bad for the business, but it's even worse if the transition affects existing services as well and creates problems there.

 Purpose and objectives

The purpose of Service Transition is to make sure that new, modified or retired services meet the business expectations documented during Service Strategy and Service Design.

Remember: retiring a service is a transition, as well as releasing a new service, or making a change to an existing one. A service retirement needs to be communicated and managed, just like a new service going live. Insourcing or outsourcing a service would also be managed as a transition.

To fulfil its role, Service Transition has a number of objectives:

- Service Transition needs to manage service changes efficiently and effectively
- it needs to manage any risks related to changes to services
- it needs to deploy releases successfully
- it needs to set expectations about how services will perform and be used
- it needs to ensure that service changes create the expected business value
- it needs to provide knowledge and information about services and service assets that make up services.

To meet its objectives, Service Transition needs to put a framework and reusable processes in place to manage service changes. Capacity and resources need to be managed during changes, and risk needs to be understood and evaluated. Service assets need to be protected, and repeatable processes must be used for activities like testing.

Scope

The adoption of Service Transition practices should lead to an organisation developing and improving its capabilities for getting new and changed services into the live environment.

Processes need to be in place for release build, test and deployment to make sure that changes do what they are supposed to do and don't create any unnecessary problems.

The scope of Service Transition also includes the retirement of services and movement of services between providers.

Requirements are mapped in Service Strategy and designed in Service Design. Service Transition then needs to transfer the service and make sure that value is delivered in Service Operation.

Service Transition needs to be aware that:

- services and processes are complex and changes are consequently more complex too
- new services and innovation need to be allowed and encouraged, but without negative effects
- services will change and evolve, and be discontinued – which all needs to be managed.

Any change to a service can initiate transition activity. Changes to the service provider's capabilities – for example moving to a new supplier – can also initiate transition processes and planning.

Service Transition uses seven processes to help it manage changes to services. Some of them are only active in Service Transition, and others support all stages of the lifecycle. Change Management, Service Asset and Configuration Management, and Knowledge Management are the Service Transition processes that are involved in the whole service lifecycle.

Transition Planning and Support, Release and Deployment Management, Service Validation and Testing, and Change Evaluation are the processes that only operate within Service Transition.

Value

Service Transition helps organisations to:

- deliver successful changes
- improve communication, expectation setting and confidence in changes
- reduce costs, delays, and timing and scheduling issues
- improve control of service assets and configuration items.

 Service Operation

Service Operation deals with the management of live services. This includes all business as usual (BAU) activities required to keep services stable on a day-to-day basis.

Purpose and objectives

The purpose of Service Operation is to undertake activities and processes to manage and deliver services at the levels agreed with business users and customers.

Service Operation manages the technology used to deliver services and collects information on performance and defined service metrics. It is vital for effective service management. Services can be well designed and transitioned smoothly, but they still need to be managed in the live environment to make sure they continue to work well.

Service Operation staff need processes and tools to support them. It is important to focus on services, not just single technology components. Any external suppliers involved in service delivery also need to be part of the Service Operation view. Tools may be used to share information between organisations involved in service delivery.

The objectives of Service Operation include:

- maintaining business confidence and satisfaction by delivering services effectively and efficiently
- minimising the effect of any service downtime for the business
- ensuring that only authorised users have access to services.

 Scope

Service Operation covers all areas of service delivery, including:

- services
- service management processes
- technology
- people.

 Value

Service Operation helps organisations to:

- reduce the impact and frequency of outages
- provide access to standard services
- provide data to justify investment.

Continual Service Improvement

 Purpose and objectives

Continual Service Improvement (CSI) interacts with all of the other phases in the lifecycle. The purpose of CSI is to identify improvements to allow IT services to stay aligned with changing business needs. Organisations should try to embed a culture of improvement in everything they do.

The objectives of CSI include:

- reviewing, analysing and prioritising improvements across the whole service lifecycle
- reviewing whether services meet their agreed targets
- identifying and implementing activities to improve service quality
- improving cost effectiveness without affecting service performance
- using quality management to support improvement
- making sure processes have clearly defined objectives and measures
- understanding what to measure, and why.

 Scope

The scope of CSI covers four main areas:

- the health of IT service management overall
- alignment of services with business needs, both now and in the future
- maturity and capability of the organisation, management, processes and people

- continual improvement of all IT services and service assets.

 Value

CSI helps organisations to:

- improve quality and reduce cost
- align IT services with business requirements
- improve services, structure, processes, capabilities and communication.

CHAPTER 4: SERVICE STRATEGY

Service Strategy theory

Purpose and objectives

Service Strategy is the centre of the service lifecycle and the axis that all the other phases revolve around. The purpose of Service Strategy is to define what a service provider needs to do to support its customer. The Service Strategy adopted must support the organisation's overall business outcomes. As part of its purpose, Service Strategy will define plans, patterns, a position and perspective for how the service provider will behave.

Service Strategy has a number of objectives. These objectives will help to define how the rest of the service lifecycle works. The Service Strategy objectives include:

- understanding what strategy is
- understanding what services are, and who the organisation's customers are
- understanding how value is created and delivered
- creating a service provision model to show how services will be delivered and funded
- understanding if the organisation is capable of delivering the strategy
- identifying opportunities to offer services and being able to act on them
- understanding what service assets make up services and managing them appropriately
- putting processes in place to make sure the strategy is delivered.

Scope

The scope of Service Strategy includes defining principles and processes for service management, which then apply to the rest of the service lifecycle. Internal and external IT service providers need a coherent strategy to make sure their services deliver value.

The scope of Service Strategy can be broken down into two areas:

- defining a strategy for how the service provider will deliver services that meet customer needs
- defining a strategy for ongoing management of services.

 Value

A well-thought-out strategy will provide benefits for an organisation. Service Strategy helps organisations to:

- offer appropriate services that meet business needs
- offer the services in a timely way
- link IT activities and assets to business outcomes to show the true value of IT
- demonstrate return on IT investment and value for money
- be seen as a trusted partner by customers.

Service Strategy concepts

These are some of the key concepts that it's important to understand for this phase of the service lifecycle.

Value creation through services

If a service doesn't deliver value to a customer, the customer won't want to use it and they certainly won't want to invest in it. A customer must understand how the service is giving them value. Services on their own aren't worth anything; they only deliver value when they are being used to deliver business outcomes and meet business objectives. If the customer can't see that a service is making them more productive, they won't see any value.

Think about these statements related to value:

- Value is defined by the customer, not the service provider.
- Services need to have an affordable mix of desirable features to attract customers.
- Value is not just measured in financial terms, services can fulfil a moral or ethical need.
- Value changes over time; what a customer values today may not be what they value tomorrow.

Customers must feel that the value of a service outweighs the cost of using the service. To be successful, an IT service provider must understand what their customer wants AND how much they are willing to pay.

IT needs to be able to articulate:

- what services it provides
- what those services achieve
- how much the services cost.

Service costs include any ongoing and maintenance costs, as well as the original purchase price of the service. This would be defined as the total cost of ownership (TCO), or total cost of utilisation (TCU).

 Quantifying the value of a service

Some services have a financial value that is easy to quantify. For example, a new automated payments system might save a customer £10,000 a month compared to the old manual payments system. Other services provide value which is intangible and harder to quantify. In this instance, the service provider needs to consider other factors such as customer expectations and perception.

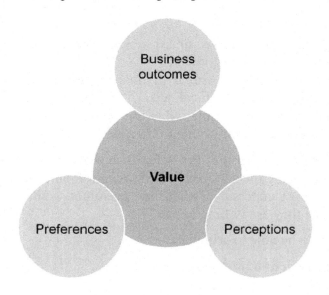

Figure 4: Components of value

Figure 4 shows the components of value. Value is more than simply what the service costs and what it does. It will be influenced by business outcomes achieved, customer preferences and the customer's perception of what was delivered. If value is intangible, it must be clearly defined and communicated. Otherwise, customers won't understand why they should purchase, or use, a service.

Remember: customer perception can be affected by many factors, not just the service provided. For example, if the relationship with the service provider is poor and getting worse, the customer might see the services in a negative light, even when they perform perfectly. The customer's perception of the service provider is influencing how they perceive the service itself. Service providers need to understand customer perception and try to influence it where possible.

 The economic value of a service

Figure 5, overleaf, provides another view of how customers perceive value.

Looking at the diagram from left to right, customers start with a reference value for a service. This could be based on things that they've heard about a service, their previous experience, or their experience of an internal, do-it-yourself arrangement.

If the service delivers benefits or gains, they will be seen as positive differences. If there is a downside to using the service, such as hidden costs or poor quality, this will be seen as a negative difference.

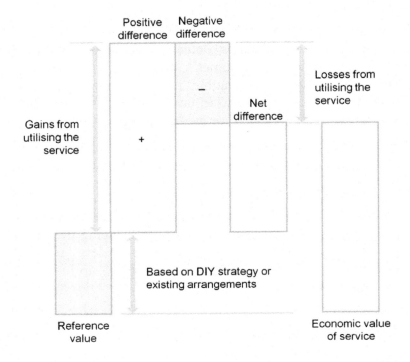

Figure 5: How customers perceive value

Comparing the reference values with the positive and negative differences associated with the service gives an overall economic value for the service. Customers weigh up the pros and cons of using a service and arrive at their own perception of value.

Remember: the customer's perception of value will change over time.

📋 *Utility and warranty*

To measure value from the customer's perspective, we can use the concepts of **utility** and **warranty.**

Utility measures whether something is **fit for purpose**. This means it offers the functionality required to deliver the service. Consider online shopping for example. Desirable functionality could include easy-to-use search tools, the ability to see previous orders, and a simple checkout process.

Warranty measures if something is **fit for use** and will meet agreed requirements. This means it offers appropriate levels of availability, continuity, security and capacity. For online shopping, warranty factors could include the website being available when needed, personal credit card details being held securely, and pages loading in an acceptable time.

Value is created when a service has the right combination of utility and warranty. If a service only offers utility or warranty, it will not meet customer requirements.

Figure 6 shows how services need to have both utility and warranty in order for value to be delivered. Utility will support the customer's performance, or remove constraints and limitations. Warranty ensures the levels of availability, capacity, security and continuity. Think of utility as WHAT we deliver to the customer and warranty as being HOW we deliver it.

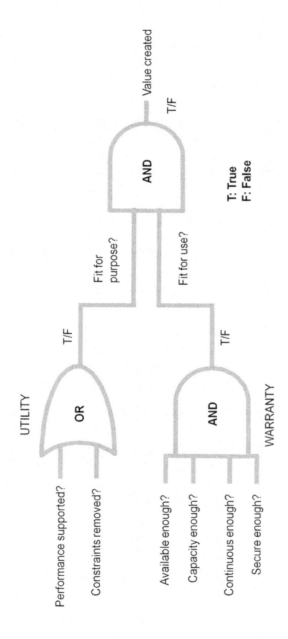

Figure 6: Services are designed, built and delivered with both utility and warranty

Risk management

Risk is defined as *'a possible event that could cause harm or loss, or affect the ability to achieve objectives. ... Risk can also be defined as uncertainty of outcome, and can be used in the context of measuring the probability of positive outcomes as well as negative outcomes.'*

Risk management needs to be embedded in service management. It must identify and assess risks, and mitigate or remove them, if necessary.

The first part of risk management involves the identification of risks. Try to get as many ideas as possible, no matter how unlikely they may sound. For example, planning for the collapse of the European currency, or for anti-capitalist riots, might have seemed unnecessary five years ago, but it is higher up the agenda now. Every risk must be documented, along with the potential consequences.

Once risks have been identified, they can be analysed to quantify their impact and probability. The impact is the effect of the risk, which could apply to services, customers, or the whole organisation. Probability measures how likely the risk is to happen. Risks can then be given a numerical ranking which allows them to be prioritised and managed. Time and effort will be devoted to risks that have the biggest impact, or highest probability.

Some risks will be defined with a 100% probability. These are not risks. They are certainties and need to be moved to an issue log and managed from there.

Any risks with a probability of zero will also be removed from the risk register, as they do not need to be managed.

Once risks are assessed and have action plans, risk management will instigate regular reviews. These make sure that actions are carried out and impact/probability values are updated as necessary. Risk will change over time.

Remember: risk management is not defined as a separate process within the ITIL core volumes. It does, however, need to be embedded right through the service lifecycle.

There is considerable guidance available related to risk management – please check the further reading list in *Chapter 13*.

 Governance

Governance defines common directions, policies and rules that apply to the business and IT. If an organisation has an existing governance structure, IT has to work within it, or it will not be aligned with the overall organisational standards.

Governance also makes sure that policies and strategy are implemented, and processes are followed. It defines roles and responsibilities, measures and reports. If any issues are identified, such as policies not being followed, then governance needs to instigate actions to resolve this.

The successful implementation of governance leads to consistency at all levels of the organisation. Strategies are used to create policies, which direct tactical and operational ways of working.

The International Standard for governance is ISO38500.

📋 *Service assets*

'A service asset is any resource or capability of a service provider.'

Services are made up of service assets. Service assets could be people, hardware, software – in fact anything that is involved in service delivery. It is important that service providers understand and manage their assets and get the best out of them.

Figure 7, below, shows some examples of capabilities and resources.

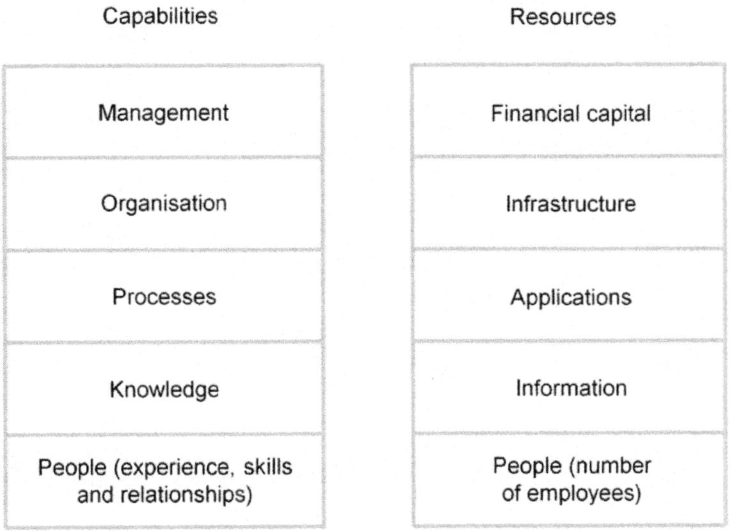

Capabilities	Resources
Management	Financial capital
Organisation	Infrastructure
Processes	Applications
Knowledge	Information
People (experience, skills and relationships)	People (number of employees)

Figure 7: Examples of capabilities and resources

Notice how people can be seen as capabilities or resources. An organisation can view people from the capabilities perspective (what they know, experience and skills, etc.) or as resources. The resource view could be, for example, a set number of staff hours required to deliver a project.

Resources can be physically accounted for and procured when needed. They are direct inputs to production. Capabilities are more intangible; they include the knowledge, processes and skills used to organise resources. Capabilities cannot produce value on their own.

🌐 *The four Ps of strategy*

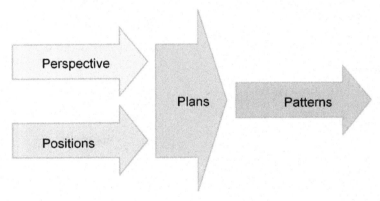

Figure 8: Perspective, positions, plans and patterns

There are four forms of strategy which need to be present when strategy is defined. This concept is based on the one introduced by Henry Mintzberg in 1987 in the 5 Ps of Strategy.

The Ps are:

- **Perspective:** describes vision and direction for an organisation.
- **Positions:** describe how a service provider will compete against other service providers.
- **Plans:** explain how the service provider will move from 'as is' to a future desired state.
- **Patterns:** describe a series of consistent actions over time.

A service provider can start with any of the Ps, and evolve the rest of them based on the results. A service provider can, for example, analyse the **patterns** of behaviour within the organisation and use this to dictate the rest of the Ps – known as an emergent strategy.

Let's take a look at an example of emergent strategy. A service provider defined its perspective as being a 'low cost service provider'.

Analysis of organisational behaviour shows that, in fact, it's working hard to provide more expensive custom solutions for customers. The customers appreciate these custom solutions and are prepared to pay more for them.

The patterns of behaviour in this organisation are not aligned with the perspective. The patterns are resulting in happy customers and increased revenue, so they can be used as a basis to redefine the perspective.

Example: An emergent strategy

The order in which the Ps are applied is not as important as actually using them.

 ## *Marketing mindset*

Service providers should aim to develop clear service definitions that can be easily explained to customers. This is the beginning of the development of a **marketing mindset.** Marketing services effectively means that customers understand them, and that the services can be aligned with customer needs.

To develop a marketing mindset, service providers need to be able to answer these questions:

- *'Who is our customer?*
- *What is our business?*
- *What does the customer value?*
- *Who depends on our services?*
- *How do they use our services?*
- *Why are they valuable to them?'*

 ## **Service Strategy process: Strategy Management for IT Services**

 ## *Purpose and objectives*

Strategy Management for IT Services (SMITS) is the process that defines and maintains the perspective, positions, plans and patterns of a service provider. SMITS makes sure the service provider can meet its customer's needs and be successful. The four Ps are driven down through the organisation, so that all teams, tasks and activities are aligned with the overall strategy.

The process objectives will include:

- understanding potential opportunities for the service provider
- identifying constraints that might limit the service provider
- understanding how the strategy needs to change over time to match evolving customer needs
- producing and maintaining plans, policies and documents related to the strategy.

 Scope

SMITS will be carried out at the executive level. The objectives of the organisation need to be defined by senior management. They can then be cascaded down through the organisation.

Every action that takes place at the tactical and operational levels should link back to the overall organisational objectives. The business strategy will shape the IT strategy, which shapes IT's tactics, plans, and procedures.

 Value

An effective SMITS process provides direction for the IT organisation. Without a clear strategy, IT may be very reactive as it tries to respond to its customers. SMITS provides a context within which to review customer requests. If customer requests are not aligned with the long-term organisational direction, they may be declined, or alternative solutions may be offered.

With SMITS, IT can invest in a balanced portfolio of services that will meet customer needs now and in the future.

 Process activities

The main Strategy Management for IT Services activities are shown in *Figure 9*, overleaf.

The process will need to:

- carry out a strategic assessment, including the service provider's internal capabilities and the external markets it operates in
- define the market and potential customers for the service provider
- identify what the service provider would need to do to be successful in each market
- establish clear organisational objectives
- evaluate and select opportunities to pursue
- define the perspective, position, plans and patterns required to support the strategy
- execute the strategy, including any supporting processes and investment
- measure the success of the strategy to guide future action.

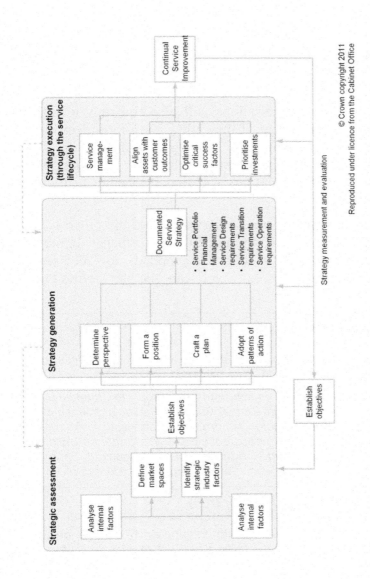

Figure 9: The strategy management process

Process considerations

SMITS can be a challenging process to implement because it requires executive involvement. If the process is carried out at a lower level of the organisation by junior employees, it will not have the authority needed and is likely to fail.

Very reactive organisations will also find this a difficult process to implement, if they allow short-term decisions to override the long-term strategy. For example, an organisation that constantly defers to customers who demand specific solutions will find it difficult to follow a strategic path.

It is important to measure the success of the process using Critical Success Factors and Key Performance Indicators. These measures should be applied to all service management processes – you can see the definitions in Table 7, below.

Critical Success Factor (CSF)
'Something that must happen if an IT service, process, plan, project or other activity is to succeed.   *Key Performance Indicators are used to measure the achievement of each Critical Success Factor. For example, a Critical Success Factor of "protect IT services when making changes" could be measured by Key Performance Indicators such as "percentage reduction of unsuccessful changes", "percentage reduction in changes causing incidents", etc.'*

Key Performance Indicator (KPI)
'A metric that is used to help manage an IT service, process, plan, project or other activity. Key Performance Indicators are used to measure the achievement of Critical Success Factors.

> Many metrics may be measured, but only the most important of these are defined as Key Performance Indicators and used to actively manage and report on the process, IT service or activity. They should be selected to ensure that efficiency, effectiveness and cost effectiveness are all managed.'

Table 7: Definitions: Critical Success Factors and Key Performance Indicators

The measures applied to SMITS must look at how well the strategy is integrated into the organisation as a whole. For example, is it reflected in the tactical and operational plans and procedures?

 Service Strategy process: Service Portfolio Management

'A Service Portfolio is a full list of services provided by an organisation, and describes services in terms of business value.'

Service providers should constantly review their services to make sure that they are still meeting customer requirements. Services have a natural lifecycle, and we should always seek opportunities to add new services – as well as retiring services that are no longer providing value.

Service Portfolio Management will help the business answer questions such as:

- Why should a customer buy a particular service?
- Why from us – as a service provider?

Asking questions like these will help businesses to make sound decisions about investment in services. Organisations also need to consider how services should be priced. What is the best way to charge for services? The Service Portfolio can help to make these decisions.

The Service Portfolio is the complete set of services managed by a service provider. It includes services that are proposed or in development, live services and retired services. The Service Portfolio Management process controls which services are added to the portfolio, and how they are tracked and managed once they are recorded in there. Only services that will add value should be added to the portfolio.

Figure 10, overleaf, shows the Service Portfolio. The portfolio maps across the whole lifecycle of service development and retirement. It includes new and conceptual services, as well as live and retired services.

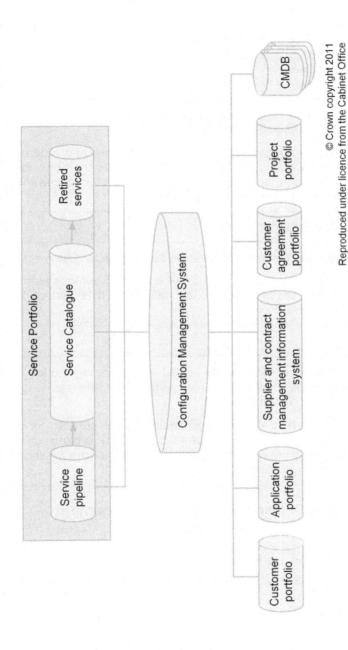

© Crown copyright 2011
Reproduced under licence from the Cabinet Office

Figure 10: The Service Portfolio

Service Portfolio Management terminology

Service pipeline
This is the section of the portfolio that contains services that are being developed and conceptual services. This would not normally be visible to customers. Some services may never complete development and progress to the Service Catalogue. This could be because their business case is not good enough to justify investment, or because they have become redundant before going live.
Service Catalogue
This contains the services that are live and visible to customers. Its contents are managed by the Service Catalogue Management process during Service Design, but ultimately it is part of the overall Service Portfolio.
Retired services
Services may be considered as retired when they are no longer available to new customers – or when they are no longer available to any customers at all. Services will be held in the retired section of the portfolio for an agreed time. This could be influenced by many organisational factors, including data retention, asset disposal, or the likelihood of a service being reinstated in the future.

Table 8: Service Portfolio Management terminology

There are many information sources linked to the Service Portfolio, such as customer portfolios and project portfolios.

The information within the Service Portfolio includes a service provider's commitments to all of its customers. It shows current contractual commitments, new services in development and improvement opportunities initiated by CSI. Third-party services may also be included – these could be visible to customers, or hidden as components of an overall service.

The services in the portfolio that are in development or conceptual show what the service provider could do if it had unlimited money and resources. This allows the service provider to prioritise where they invest and get maximum value.

The Service Portfolio needs to be properly governed. Entry and exit to each area can only happen if funding and plans are in place, and business value has been articulated. If a service doesn't have defined plans and funding, resources will not be allocated to it, as there is a risk the service will not deliver value.

The Service Portfolio helps service providers make sure they have services in place to meet customer needs – now and in the future.

A service can exist in more than one part of the portfolio at once. For example, v1.0 of a service may be retired. The next version, v2.0, is live, and v3.0 is in development.

 Purpose and objectives

The purpose of Service Portfolio Management is to make sure a service provider has the right mix of services to meet customer requirements. The investment made in IT needs to be in balance with the services offered.

The process will track what investment is made in services, and then track the services themselves to make sure they deliver a return on investment. As part of this process, all services in the portfolio will be clearly defined and linked to the business outcomes they support.

The rest of the lifecycle activities (including design, transition and operation) will be driven by the service definition and the desired value.

The process objectives include:

- providing a mechanism to help service providers decide what services to offer to their customers
- maintaining a definitive portfolio of services
- providing a mechanism to show how services support organisational strategy and business outcomes
- controlling what services are offered and when
- tracking service investment and the return on investment
- analysing which services should be retired and when.

Scope

Service Portfolio Management includes all services, whether planned, live or in development. New services are linked to business outcomes, so that investment can be compared to returns. Live services are also linked to business outcomes, and retired when they no longer deliver value.

Value

The main value of Service Portfolio Management is the way it controls what services are offered. Services are only added to the portfolio if they have a business case and are linked to business outcomes. This means that no money or resources are wasted delivering services that are not needed or do not deliver value.

Concept: types of investment

Investment in services will be dictated by organisational priorities. If a service isn't aligned with the current and future organisational direction, it is unlikely to receive any investment.

Services will be placed into one of three strategic categories:

- **Run the business:** an organisation in this mode will prioritise investment to focus on maintaining the current service operation. Existing services will be maintained, but there will be minimal investment in new services.
- **Grow the business:** investment here aims to increase the scope of the organisation's services. Investment in existing services will be used to broaden their capabilities. There will be minimal investment in new services.
- **Transform the business:** investment here will move the organisation into new markets. There will be investment in new services to support the move into new markets.

The organisational strategy will help to decide how investment is split between the categories. The investment decisions will be revisited regularly, as organisational priorities and customer requirements evolve.

🌐 *Process activities*

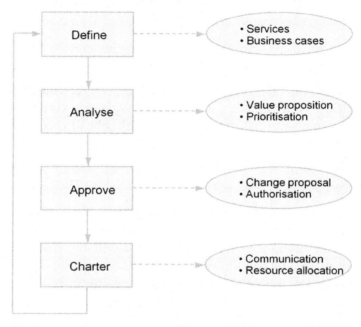

Figure 11: Phases of Service Portfolio Management

Service Portfolio Management has four main phases of activity:

- **Define:** this phase documents and understands new and existing services. Each service must have an associated business case.
- **Analyse:** services are analysed to see if they will provide value, or continue to provide value, and whether supply is meeting customer demand.

- **Approve:** all services have to be approved. Approval guarantees the investment and resources needed to deliver the service.
- **Charter:** the project authorisation, scope, terms and references are documented in a charter. This is a formal process used to communicate investment decisions to stakeholders.

🌐 *Process considerations*

Service Portfolio Management relies on accurate information to be successful. If new services are commissioned and the process is not informed, the Service Portfolio will be out of date very quickly.

It is important to make sure the process is involved in the full lifecycle of services all the way through to retirement. It's dangerous to focus solely on new services. Many organisations continue to spend money and time on old services that don't deliver value and could be retired.

Service Portfolio Management also needs to have close links to the business. A service that delivers value is a service that meets business objectives. Service value can only be assessed if Service Portfolio Management actually understands the business objectives. A poor relationship with the business will be very damaging for this process.

The historical relationship between IT and the business will also affect Service Portfolio Management. It will be difficult to maintain the focus on service value, if there are customers in the organisation who expect to demand a new service and have it delivered 'because that's the way things have always been'.

Service Strategy process: Financial Management for IT Services

Financial Management for IT Services (FMITS) is the process that provides information about the value of services – and their cost.

Think about an IT service. Let's take e-mail as an example. The service assets for e-mail include servers, software, back-up resources, networks, and desktop hardware amongst other things. However, many of these components are not used by the e-mail service alone. Other applications will share the same servers and other services use the same network. So, how can we determine the actual cost of providing the e-mail service?

If we can't determine or provide the cost of the service, how can we make decisions about whether or not e-mail delivers value?

This is where FMITS really helps.

 Purpose and objectives

FMITS secures the funding needed to design, develop and deliver services that support the organisational strategy. It will make sure a service provider can afford to deliver the services it offers, and balance service cost with service quality.

The process objectives include:

- implementing a framework to identify, manage and communicate the cost of service provision
- securing funding for services throughout their lifecycle

- evaluating the financial impact of new or changed strategies
- balancing income and expenses
- managing assets
- providing financial reports
- executing financial policies and plans
- forecasting and budgeting financial requirements
- accounting for money spent on services
- creating a fair and appropriate charging mechanism, if required.

 Scope

Most organisations already have some form of corporate financial management in place. Financial Management for IT Services needs specialised skills, as well as the expected accountancy skills. Process staff must understand technology as well as finance and business considerations. Cost-accounting skills are needed to provide detailed information to management.

IT's financial policies and practices need to follow the organisational guidelines and standard practices. This will allow IT and the business to communicate easily about financial matters.

FMITS includes three main processes:

- **Budgeting:** predicts and controls income and expenditure for the financial period.
- **Accounting:** tracks how money is spent during the financial period.
- **Charging:** bills customers for services provided, if required.

These processes all have two cycles of activity. On an annual basis, projections and plans are produced. On an operational basis, costs are monitored and checked and bills are issued (if relevant). This will normally happen monthly or quarterly.

 Value

An effective FMITS process allows a service provider to comply with any internal, regulatory or legislative requirements. Accurate budgets and forecasts will reduce unplanned expenditure, and will lead to better decisions about whether to invest in IT and when.

For internal IT departments, FMITS allows them to show the business how money is invested in services. This can prevent IT being seen as a 'black hole' where money is pumped every financial year for no real return.

 Concept: business case

A business case is *'justification for a significant item of expenditure'*. It projects the likely consequences of a business action, and is used to make a reasoned argument for investment. Business cases are used to justify new investment and can be an integral part of Change Management and change proposals.

Most organisations will have their own templates for business cases. These will typically include:

- **introduction**: setting the scene
- **methods and assumptions**: for example, how analysis was carried out and any missing information

- **business impacts of the proposed action**: these will be both financial and non-financial
- **risks and contingencies**
- **recommendations:** including costed options where appropriate.

The FMITS process will help an organisation to produce realistic business cases. If business cases are regularly presented with inaccurate financial projections, it's very difficult for senior management to make sensible decisions about investment. They will not trust the information they receive in business cases, and will rely on other sources instead.

 Process activities

Figure 12, overleaf, shows the main FMITS process activities, split into the accounting, budgeting and charging areas.

All service providers have to create budgets and account for money spent. Charging for services is optional. Service providers with external customers must charge for their services to generate revenue, but internal service providers may be allocated central funding by the business instead.

Some organisations implement an internal charging scheme where money is transferred between departments in a business. This will be a senior management decision – it will create an extra administrative overhead, but it can help to clearly demonstrate the cost of using IT services for each business department.

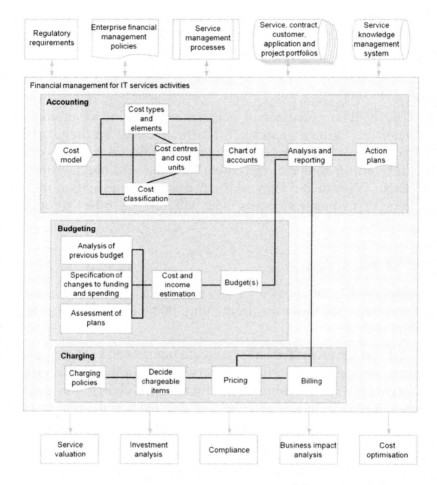

Figure 12: Major inputs, outputs and activities of Financial Management for IT Services

Some organisations implement a notional charging scheme, where invoices are issued, but no money changes hands. This can help business units to understand the true cost of IT services, without the organisation needing to introduce any formal way of moving money between budgets.

Process considerations

FMITS will be implemented differently in different types of service providers.

- Type 1 Service Providers are closely linked to a single business unit. They may not charge for their services, and their financial policies and budgets will be set by the business unit they are linked to.
- Type 2 Service Providers serve multiple business units from the same organisation. They will have more financial autonomy, and may charge for their services through an internal charging mechanism.
- Type 3 Service Providers are external or third-party service providers – their customers are from different organisations. They will charge for their services, and their profitability and perceived value will be key to their success.

Some organisations believe that their overall organisational financial management process is sufficient, and do not invest in Financial Management for IT Services. This is a mistake. FMITS will break down the cost of IT services in more detail than the organisational financial management process, which will lead to better IT investment decisions in the future.

FMITS can be a complicated process to implement. General IT staff will not usually have the skills required, so they will need training or support from staff with financial qualifications and experience.

Many organisations are constantly trying to reduce the cost of providing IT services. FMITS should focus on cost **optimisation** rather than cost cutting. Cost optimisation looks at the most efficient way to provide the services required by the business, not cutting a set percentage of the IT spend year on year. Costs can only be cut so far before service quality suffers.

Service Strategy process: Demand Management

Demand Management is the process that tries to understand how customers will use services. Poorly managed demand is a risk for service providers, because it can affect service performance. If a service provider has too much unused capacity, they will not be efficient and will waste resources. If they do not have enough capacity, their services might fail. Customers will not expect to pay for idle capacity unless it is a defined part of the service. For example, a redundant server might be part of a service continuity solution.

Demand must exist to 'pull' capacity. Having capacity will not magically create demand.

Purpose and objectives

Demand Management exists to understand, anticipate and influence customer demand for services. This could mean steering customers away from an over-used service, or towards an under-used one.

The process works closely with Capacity Management and is active at every stage of the service lifecycle, making sure services are designed, built, tested and delivered in a way that meets business demand.

The process objectives include:

- understanding and analysing patterns of business activity
- building profiles of demand from users, including different user groups and types of user
- making sure services are designed to meet demand
- anticipating and managing any issues related to demand
- continually reviewing services and adapting them where necessary as demand levels change.

 Scope

Demand Management is active during the whole service lifecycle. Many service management processes are defined and documented in one core volume and one lifecycle stage, but then continue to have an active role in other stages. Demand Management continually analyses customer behaviour and business trends to try to predict demand, providing valuable information to Capacity Management during design activities.

Value

Demand Management helps to optimise the resources used to deliver a service, balancing the cost of delivery against the business outcomes supported. There will be fewer 'surprises' and fewer service failures related to fluctuations in demand.

The outputs from Demand Management will help Service Design to create services that will meet business needs from day one. Service Operation uses the outputs to create support rotas and understand when service usage will peak and trough.

 Concept: supply and demand

Demand Management matches supply to demand.

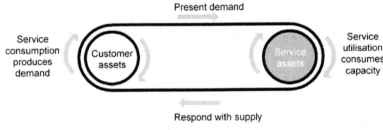

Figure 13: Tight coupling between demand, capacity and supply

The process needs to understand what demand will be presented and how this will affect service assets and available capacity.

Remember: service providers cannot stockpile spare capacity, so they need to optimise how they use their service assets.

 Concept: patterns of business activity

Customers don't use services in the same way every day. Sometimes services will have a lot of use during specific periods, for example, e-mail systems might experience heavy usage on a Monday morning when staff start to clear their in-boxes. At other times, usage drops and the load on the service reduces.

Service providers need to understand how customers use their services. If they deliver a service that cannot cope with the normal variations in customer activity, it will not meet customer needs.

Service providers need to understand their customer's patterns of business activity (PBA). A PBA is *'a workload profile of one or more business activities. PBAs are used to help the IT service provider understand and plan for different levels of business activity.'*

PBAs are driven by customer demand. This can be difficult to predict, but not impossible. Studying how the business works, peak hours, customer profiles, service packages, etc. will all help to build a picture of the demand a service is likely to experience.

Service providers need to work hard to understand PBAs and may even try to influence them. They can use different methods and techniques to try to change how customers use services – rather than assuming a PBA is fixed and cannot be changed.

For example, peak and off-peak charging might be used to try to change the hours that services are accessed. If the service is very expensive to use during peak hours, demand will shift to off-peak hours when the service is cheaper to use. The service provider benefits because they do not have to cope with such wild fluctuations in demand, and the customer should benefit from a more reliable, accessible service.

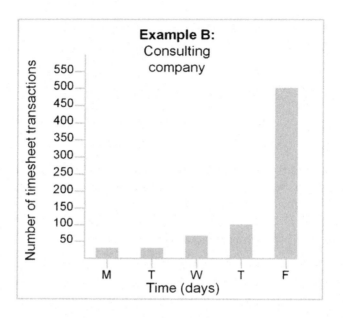

Figure 14: Examples of patterns of business activity (extract)

This diagram shows an example of a PBA for a timesheet system used by consultants. It is not used much during the week, but on a Friday, the usage surges as the consultants all complete their timesheets for the week. The service provider needs to have enough capacity to meet this demand, but also needs to try to avoid having lots of spare capacity during the rest of the week.

They could, for example, divert capacity from a service that isn't used much on a Friday afternoon and use it to support the timesheet system temporarily.

For every PBA, critical information needs to be documented, including:

- **classification:** including the type of pattern and the workload supported
- **attributes:** such as volume, frequency, location or duration
- **requirements:** such as performance or availability
- **service asset requirements:** what is needed to fulfil demand?

 Process activities

Demand Management will draw information from many sources to help it build patterns of business activity and profiles of users. The process will make sure service offerings can meet customer demand, and will continue to track operational demand and try to forecast any changes.

 Process considerations

Demand Management can only work with input from the customer. Some demand is regular and easy to predict (for example, fewer users in the office during public holidays). Other demand is activity-related or generated by a one-off event, such as a marketing campaign generating large amounts of traffic to a website.

Demand Management needs to work with the business to get visibility of any upcoming marketing activities, or other business events, that may generate additional demand. The process owner might attend departmental meetings, or request access to schedules for marketing campaigns or e-mail campaigns. Business Relationship Management may be able to support Demand Management here.

It is important to remember that Demand Management can be a cost-saving process. Influencing demand to prevent service overload can delay the need to invest in new services or extra capacity. Resources can be reconfigured temporarily to support increased demand.

 Service Strategy process: Business Relationship Management

Business Relationship Management (BRM) is the link between the customer and the service provider at the strategic and tactical level. It exists to help the service provider deliver what the customer wants, and respond to any customer dissatisfaction.

 Purpose and objectives

The purpose of Business Relationship Management covers two main areas:

- establishing and maintaining a relationship between the customer and the service provider
- identifying customer needs and making sure they are met by the service provider.

Customer needs will change over time, so this is not a one-off exercise. To meet its objectives, the process needs to:

- build a good relationship between the customer and the service provider

- identify changes to the customer environment that could affect services or requirements
- be aware of technology changes that could affect the customer
- establish and communicate requirements for new or changed services
- create a process for mediating and managing complaints
- create a process for logging, distributing and publicising compliments.

 ## *Scope*

When the service provider is part of the same organisation as the customer, Business Relationship Management will usually happen at the management level.

If the service provider is external, there may be a dedicated business relationship manager role, or a team of account managers.

Internal service providers work hard to meet business goals and objectives. External providers try to maximise contract value through satisfied customers.

BRM focuses on making sure services meet customer needs. The process needs to understand what is currently being offered, and how the services support business outcomes. If the customer is not satisfied, the process will work with customers to put a plan in place to remedy the situation.

BRM depends on other service management processes to be effective. For example, Service Portfolio Management helps it to understand what services are offered to customers and what might be offered in the future.

Most service management processes focus on individual services. BRM is different, as it focuses on customers. However, it still needs to understand the services on offer – just as other service management processes need to understand what the customer wants.

BRM is concerned with the design and build of services, not just their operation. Many complaints about live services could have been avoided if the design and transition activities were carried out differently.

 Concept: Service Level Management and Business Relationship Management

Service Level Management (SLM) and Business Relationship Management are often confused. SLM is the process that agrees and manages the Service Level Agreements negotiated with customers. It is important to understand the difference between the two processes: Business Relationship Management's main purpose is to maintain the overall relationship with the customer; SLM has a slightly different view, focusing on negotiating specific targets for individual services.

Business Relationship Management is strategic and tactical. SLM is tactical and operational. BRM will focus on required utility and warranty, and SLM will focus on the warranty agreed.

The way the two processes are measured is also different. Business Relationship Management is measured on customer satisfaction, while Service Level Management is measured on the achievement of service performance targets.

Value

BRM provides the link between service provider and customer, focused on building a solid, lasting relationship. Many relationships break down because of lack of communication – service providers need to spend time and energy trying to stop this happening.

An effective BRM process means the service provider has more chance of meeting customer requirements, both now and in the future. If the customer doesn't trust the service provider and won't share any information with them, it's very difficult for the service provider to deliver good services.

 Process activities

Figure 15, overleaf, shows the main Business Relationship Management process activities. You can see the process is active right through the service lifecycle.

The process will maintain a customer portfolio that includes details of all the service provider's customers. This will be linked to a customer agreement portfolio that details the different contracts, or agreements, in place with each customer. The process must understand customer requirements for services. It will measure customer satisfaction and react to any changes.

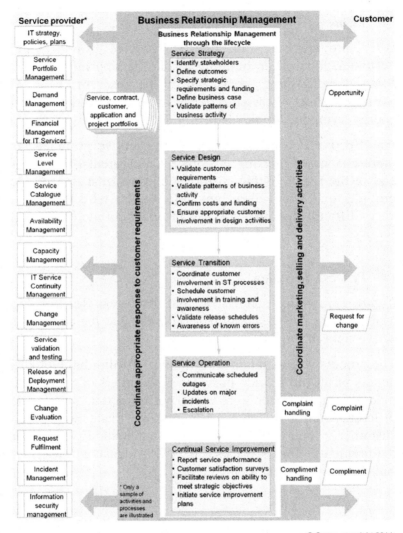

Figure 15: Business Relationship Management process activities

Process considerations

Business Relationship Management should not be implemented as a quick fix if customer satisfaction is low. To be effective, the process needs to be involved right through the service lifecycle, including during Service Design. The process should be proactive and involved early in the service lifecycle, not brought in at the end when things go wrong.

If a service provider has a poor relationship with its customers, the process might struggle to improve the situation immediately. Patience is required – things will only improve when the customer trusts the service provider and starts to share information.

BRM will only be effective if it is seen as a neutral process. If the customer believes the process always favours IT, or vice versa, it will not be effective. BRM staff need to be ethical and responsible. Sometimes they will have to deliver tough messages, but it's better to tell a hard truth than to mislead either party.

For many organisations, relationship problems develop because the customer can't explain what they want in IT terms, and see the IT staff as speaking 'techie speak'. BRM can provide a useful translation service.

 Putting Service Strategy to work

Here are some areas to consider during strategic planning in your organisation.

Strategy and strategic planning have to happen at the right level. They will only be effective if they are set by senior executives and cascaded down through the organisation.

The service management strategy has to be aligned with the overall organisational strategy. If IT is pursuing different goals to the rest of the organisation, then services are very unlikely to meet customer needs.

Strategy also has to be communicated to be effective. A strategy is not a document that is written and stuffed in a cupboard until next year. It has to be shared and understood at all levels of the organisation. Asking operational staff about their understanding of the organisational strategy is a good way of judging its effectiveness.

Strategy is not set in stone and inflexible. The internal and external environment may change significantly after the strategy is drawn up and agreed. It is important that the strategy adopted can flex and adapt to changes that affect the organisation.

It is easy to tell if a strategy is working – is everyone doing it? If the strategy adopted cannot be met with existing resources and capabilities, it will be circumvented by the lower levels of the organisation. This may be a sign that the strategy is too ambitious, or constraints need to be removed.

A new strategy will take time to be adopted. Executives may decide how they want the organisation to behave, but this will take time to filter down and change ways of working. Executives need to be patient and accept that large changes take time – a revolutionary new strategy will not be completely implemented by the end of the week.

CHAPTER 5: SERVICE DESIGN

 Service Design theory

Once a strategy has been defined and communicated, services can be designed to meet the strategic objectives. The purpose of the Service Design stage of the lifecycle is to design services that fulfil the strategic objectives, which are based on business requirements.

IT processes, practices and policies also need to be designed to make sure that services are high quality, cost effective, and meet customer needs.

The main objective of Service Design is to deliver a service which works. By 'works', we mean that it won't need lots of improvement when it is live, reducing the cost of delivering the service.

All Service Design activities must have continual improvement embedded in them, so that solutions and designs are always getting better.

 Scope

The scope of Service Design includes the design of appropriate and innovative services that meet business needs now and in the future. This can be difficult to achieve as IT needs to work with the business and make some educated guesses about what future requirements will be. There are a number of Service Design processes and concepts that support this. The actual service designs that are possible will be influenced by requirements, business benefits and constraints.

Value

Effective Service Design practices help organisations to:

- improve service quality, so that services meet business needs from the moment they go live
- make sure service implementations go well – consistently
- make sure service performance is in line with agreed business requirements
- reduce service cost including the cost of redesign and rework
- improve governance and decision making
- improve service management and process design.

 **Service Design concepts**

These are some of the key concepts that it is important to understand for this phase of the service lifecycle.

 The four Ps

Be careful! Don't get these confused with the four Ps we looked at as part of Service Strategy.

The four Ps of Service Design are the four areas that need to be considered together to design a successful service management practice.

The four Ps is a model that is used to make sure services and processes are designed effectively and will be fully integrated into an organisation. If any 'P' is missing, the design is more likely to fail.

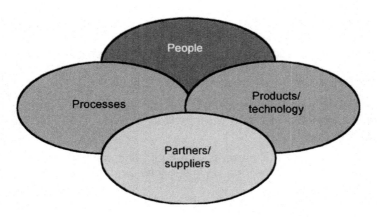

Figure 16: The four Ps

People
People considerations are vital for all service management initiatives, projects and enhancements.
This P would include education and awareness, communication and expectation setting. If people understand what changes are happening and why, they are much less likely to resist the change.
Processes
Processes need to be defined and documented. If processes are not documented, inconsistencies will develop over time as people adapt them. It is hard to track a process effectively if it is not documented.
This P includes understanding the process objectives, creating process documentation and defining process KPIs and metrics.

Partners
Very few organisations work in isolation. They use third parties who supply goods and services – from consultants and contractors through to software and tooling suppliers. We need to involve our partners in our vision. For example, partners often provide data to us, which is vital for our service measurements. If we don't involve our partners, we could find we have gaps in our ability to measure our own services and the value they provide.
Products
This P includes the tools or products that we use to help us provide, manage and measure our services. Without products, we would need costly extra resources to manually replace what our tools do for us.

Table 9: The four Ps

 The five design aspects

Service Design has five aspects. Used together, they support a holistic approach to design, which makes sure nothing is left out. Many organisations have seen the negative effect of projects that develop a service in isolation, only to find it will not integrate with other services, or areas of the infrastructure.

Aspect 1: design of service solutions

Service solutions must be designed using documented and agreed business requirements – not based on what the service provider thinks the customer wants.

Before a new service is designed, existing services must be analysed to see if they can meet the requirement, instead of designing something new.

During the design of service solutions, service providers or project teams will need to balance business requirements and the organisational strategy, available resources and timescales. Documenting and agreeing the business requirements makes sure all parties start with a clear picture of what the service should do, and prevents arguments when the service goes live about what was really wanted.

 Aspect 2: designing management information systems and tools

Management information systems are used to support and automate processes. This automation supports the management of services throughout the lifecycle, by making reporting and monitoring much more simple and less labour-intensive.

The overall organisational management system will include individual service management systems, such as the Information Security Management System and the quality management system.

This aspect of Service Design also includes the design of the Service Portfolio. Although the Service Portfolio is used during Service Strategy, it's designed by Service Design.

The structure of the Service Portfolio needs to support the process purpose and objectives. It must allow services to be tracked through their lifecycle, so that their value can be clearly identified.

 Aspect 3: design of technology and management architectures

Architectures provide high-level guidance and blueprints for teams undertaking design activities.

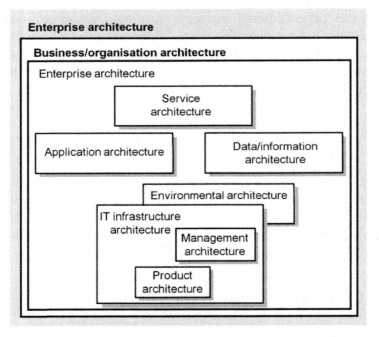

Figure 17: Enterprise architecture

Organisations need to be confident that any new or changed service will interface with existing services and meets their long-term technical plans. Making architectures available to design teams will provide this confidence.

Figure 17 shows how the overall enterprise architecture will influence architectures at other levels of the organisation, for example, the data/information architecture defines data assets and how they are managed. This will ensure consistency and ease of integration at all levels and for all service components.

Technology architectures will address all areas of IT, including applications, servers, networks, storage devices, and much more.

Management architectures will be either proprietary, or best of breed.

- **Proprietary architecture:** products and tools are selected from a single supplier who can meet most of the organisation's needs. This makes implementation and integration simpler, but may require some compromises if all functionality is not available.
- **Best of breed architecture:** tools are selected from a number of different suppliers to allow all requirements to be met. This reduces the amount of compromises that have to be made, but will have an impact on the amount of supplier management required, as well as making the implementation more complicated.

 Aspect 4: design of processes

Every new or changed service will require underpinning service management processes. All of these areas will be considered, documented, agreed and communicated as the process is designed:

- inputs and outputs
- process objectives and scope
- roles, including the process owner, manager and practitioners
- process controls
- process documentation
- responsibilities and skills
- metrics and measurements.

Existing processes may need to be adjusted or altered, so that they can support new or changed services. These changes should be considered before the new or changed service is released to the live environment.

 Aspect 5: design of measurement methods and metrics

Processes and services need to be measured to assess whether they are performing as they should. As part of the design process, measurements and metrics need to be defined. Existing toolsets are checked to see if they can provide the required monitoring – if not, a new toolset may need to be included and budgeted for as part of the design activities.

Measurements can change behaviour – not always in a positive way. Too much focus on meeting one target can lead to a drop in performance in other areas. It's very important to choose metrics carefully, and think about the effect that they will have on the teams responsible for meeting them.

Metrics should align with the business objectives for a new or changed service. If metrics aren't telling the service provider anything useful, the effort put into capturing them is wasted.

Process metrics typically focus on four areas:

- **Progress:** measuring milestones and deliverables in the capability of the process.
- **Compliance:** does the process comply with governance requirements and regulatory requirements, and do people comply with the process?
- **Effectiveness:** does the process do what it is meant to do? Is it accurate?
- **Efficiency:** this measures the process productivity, including speed, throughput and resource utilisation.

As services and processes mature, their measurements and metrics will evolve. When a process is first implemented, simple metrics may be used to check if it works or not. As the process matures, more complex metrics can be applied to check how efficient it is and whether it is improving over time.

📋 Service Design process: Service Level Management

Service Level Agreements (SLAs) are commonly used to set customer expectations about the level of service they will receive.

Service Level Management (SLM) is responsible for working with the customer to define the service level targets that are used to measure performance and value.

Purpose and objectives

The purpose of Service Level Management is to make sure that all current and planned services are delivered to agreed, achievable targets. To do this, Service Level Management will negotiate, agree, monitor, report and review IT service targets and achievements. They will also take corrective action when targets are not achieved, and initiate improvements to services.

The objectives of Service Level Management include:

- managing the agreement and review of service targets
- working with Business Relationship Management to improve the overall customer relationship
- making sure all IT services have targets in place, not just a handful of services
- monitoring and trying to improve customer satisfaction
- making sure IT and the customer have a clear and unambiguous understanding of what level of service will be delivered
- identifying cost-effective service improvements and managing them via a Service Improvement Plan (SIP).

Service Level Agreements are not a stick for the customer to beat IT with, or a document for IT to hide behind. They represent a common understanding of what the customer needs, and what IT believes it can deliver.

If the customer or the service provider doesn't participate fully in SLA negotiation, the document produced will be of little value. Both parties need to sign up to the SLA and use it to guide service provision. If service targets are not being met, the parties need to work together to understand why, and how the situation can be improved.

📋 Scope

The scope of Service Level Management is to be a path for communication between IT and the business. Although the Service Level Management process roles are often part of the IT organisation structure, the process needs to be neutral and shouldn't be seen as favouring IT or the business – just like Business Relationship Management during Service Strategy.

Service Level Management includes current and future services, making sure that customer expectations are realistic. For new services, Service Level Management will work with the customer to produce a set of agreed Service Level Requirements. These document what the customer wants, and are signed off so that everyone understands what has been agreed. Service Level Requirements make sure all services and service components are aligned with business needs.

Every IT service should have targets documented as part of the service's design. If we do not understand our customer's objectives and requirements and translate them into targets, then how can we possibly design a solution that meets these targets?

Service Level Management has a major role to play during Service Design when targets are agreed, but it is also responsible for providing ongoing measurement and reporting once the service is live and operational.

In addition to agreeing targets for new services, Service Level Management needs to make sure that existing services won't be affected by any changes. A new service might mean another service starts to perform poorly, so this needs to be predicted, understood and managed.

Part of the ongoing role of Service Level Management after Service Design is to monitor and measure live services and provide reports to stakeholders and customers.

It is also worth considering what is NOT in the scope for Service Level Management. This includes:

- agreeing detailed functionality requirements for a new or changed service
- carrying out technical activities to make sure targets are met
- negotiating supplier contracts – this is done by Supplier Management. Service Level Management needs to know if there are any third parties involved in service delivery so that they can be monitored, but they won't agree the actual contract.

Value

Service Level Management provides value to IT and the business. Better communication between the two parties at the service level will lead to greater trust. The business will be more willing to supply information to IT about what it needs, so that IT can become a better service provider.

Effective SLM will provide the business with management information about service performance. The process will also provide feedback to the business when a service target is breached (or almost breached) and help to produce a plan to prevent the situation recurring.

Concept: Service Level Requirements (SLRs)

One of the earliest activities for Service Level Management is to collect the customer's Service Level Requirements, or SLRs.

Service Level Requirements are defined as *'a customer requirement for an aspect of an IT service. SLRs are based on business objectives and used to negotiate agreed service level targets'.*

Collecting customer SLRs can be a challenging process. For example, the customer may not be able to articulate what they want in technical terms. Or, they may ask for extremely high levels of service that aren't cost-justified, or the current infrastructure cannot provide. SLRs must be aligned to the business criticality of the service. If a service is not business critical, then the business should not really be asking for extremely high levels of service – and it probably won't want to pay for them.

It can be useful for the service level manager to attend the SLR negotiation with a solid idea of what IT is capable of providing. This should be done in consultation with all other service management processes – for example – Capacity and Availability Management. From here, the service level manager can then help the customer to draft reasonable SLRs that the service provider will be able to meet.

 Concept: Service Level Agreement (SLA)

An SLA is the instrument that Service Level Management uses to document the targets they have agreed with the customer.

An SLA is *'an agreement between an IT service provider and a customer'.*

It provides a description of the service, the actual targets and its associated reports and reporting cycle.

Service Level Agreements should be reviewed regularly (usually at least annually) to help ensure the targets are still relevant.

A typical SLA will include:

*   service description
*   service targets, including availability, security, service hours, continuity and performance
*   support arrangements
*   reporting schedule
*   Change Management process
*   contacts and escalation paths
*   signatories.

 Concept: types of Service Level Agreement

In any organisation, different types of SLA can be used, depending on the nature of the service and the type of customers.

The service level manager will be responsible for deciding which agreement type is most suitable, based on business needs. A typical organisation will implement a mixture of SLA types to address all customer needs across all services.

*   **Service-based SLA:** this is an SLA for a single service that applies to all customers. For example, an organisation's e-mail service is usually available to everyone, so it's easier to create a single SLA. There are

some challenges associated with this type of SLA – for example, it can be challenging to define the signatory for each customer group, and it may become apparent that one customer requires a higher level of service. Differentiated offerings can be created using service classes, such as bronze, silver and gold options, to help meet different customer needs.

- **Customer-based SLA:** this is the opposite of a service-based agreement – it is an agreement with a single customer covering all of the services that they use. Customers will often prefer this type of SLA as it is tailored to their needs and excludes any services that are not relevant. The challenges associated with this type of SLA include making sure that the customer representative truly represents the views of the customer group, and preventing duplication when there are many customer-based agreements referencing the same service.

- **Multi-level SLA:** organisations also have the option to choose a multi-level structure. This avoids duplication and reduces the number of updates required, but can only be effective when based on an accurate Service Catalogue and Configuration Management System.

Let's take an example of a multi-level SLA. Figure 18, overleaf, shows a three-level SLA, which comprises:

- **Corporate level:** covers generic targets and issues that apply to all customers. This might cover areas such as standard service hours, which change fairly infrequently.

- **Customer level:** covers targets or issues for a customer group across all services – for example, one group may require out-of-hours support.

- **Service level:** covers issues or targets related to a service for a specific customer group – for example, one group may need 24x7 support for one particular service.

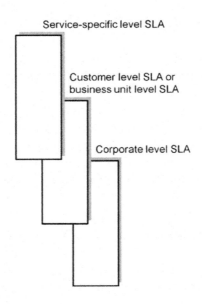

Figure 18: Multi-level SLAs

Organisations need to develop templates for each type of SLA that they intend to use. This can be done at the same time as the first SLAs are being drafted.

Once the templates are created, they can be stored in the Service Knowledge Management System, so that they are easily accessible when required. This will improve consistency and reduce the amount of time it takes to create future SLAs.

If a target can't be measured, it should be excluded from the SLA. Imagine a service review meeting between the service level manager and the customer. The customer claims that recent service performance has been terrible. The service provider believes the performance has been exceptional. Without measures and metrics, neither party can prove their point. Targets that can't be measured are meaningless.

Concept: Service Level Agreement monitoring chart

A Service Level Agreement monitoring chart (SLAM chart) is used by Service Level Management to show customers how a service has performed.

A SLAM chart is often colour-coded, so that customers can see at a glance which targets are being met and which have been breached, or came close to a breach. SLAM charts are often based around a traffic light system: red for targets that have been breached, amber for targets that have come close to a breach, and green for areas that are performing within acceptable parameters.

SLAM charts and other service level reports will feed into the regular service reviews held by Service Level Management.

Have a go: why not create a SLAM chart for one of your services? You will find many examples on the Internet.

Concept: contract/underpinning contract

Third-party suppliers may be utilised to meet some or all of the targets in an SLA. For example, a third party might provide break/fix services related to printers or desktop PCs. The service customer will enter into an SLA with their service provider. The service provider will then use underpinning contracts to manage the third-party suppliers involved in service delivery.

A contract is *'a legally binding agreement between two or more parties'*.

It is important to note that Service Level Management is not responsible for negotiating these contracts – this will be done by Supplier Management in consultation with Service Level Management.

For the end user receiving the service, service provision should be seamless. If a supplier is not performing well, Service Level Management needs to recognise this and do something about it. It's not acceptable to just 'blame the supplier'.

 ### Concept: Operational Level Agreement (OLA)

There may be more than one internal team involved in the delivery of a service. Think about getting ready for a new user joining an organisation: facilities may provide furniture, Access Management will set up their accounts, communications teams may connect their phone, and so on. If one team isn't doing its job properly or on time, then the service provider might fail its overall SLA target.

An Operational Level Agreement is *'an agreement between an IT service provider and another part of the same organisation. It supports the IT service provider's delivery of IT services to customers and defines the goods or services to be provided and the responsibilities of both parties. For example, there could be an Operational Level Agreement between the IT service provider and a procurement department to obtain hardware in agreed times.'*

OLAs are used to provide targets for and manage the different teams involved in service provision. The targets in the OLAs need to underpin the targets in the SLA.

Remember: OLAs will be used to manage internal teams. Contracts will be used to manage external suppliers.

SLAs, OLAs and contracts will normally be written in different types of language:

- SLAs need to be written in business language, so that the customer understands what they are signing and isn't confused by too much technical information.
- OLAs can be written in technical language, as they are often between different areas of the service provider and describe technical activities.
- Contracts will be written in legal language, as they are between two separate organisations.

 Concept: process interfaces

To be successful, the Service Level Management process relies on other service management processes. The main interfaces for this process are detailed below.

Service Strategy interfaces

Business Relationship Management: as we've already mentioned, this process helps to make sure that SLM fully understands business and customer needs.

Financial Management for IT Services: this process helps SLM to understand the cost of delivering the level of service requested by the customer. The customer can then make an informed decision about whether they are willing to pay for the level of service, or whether they will accept a reduced level of service for a lesser cost. FMITS will also help SLM to compare predicted service costs with actual service costs to help improve the accuracy of forecasts.

 Service Design interfaces

Service Catalogue Management: without an accurate catalogue of services, it's very hard for SLM to identify where SLAs needs to be created. Service Catalogue Management also helps SLM to identify how services fit together, and which customers are using which services and need to be engaged with.

Supplier Management: third-party suppliers may provide services that fulfil the agreed service level targets. Supplier Management supports SLM by making sure the right contracts are in place and suppliers are delivering the required level of service.

Availability, Capacity, IT Service Continuity Management and Information Security Management: these processes all help SLM to deliver realistic SLAs with achievable targets. They will assess Service Level Requirements for their own areas of responsibility and feed information back to SLM. On an ongoing basis they will carry out activities that make sure targets continue to be met.

Design Coordination: this process uses information from SLM to help coordinate design activities. The requirements collected by SLM help Design Coordination to understand what design activities need to be completed.

 Service Operation interfaces

Incident Management: incident data provided to SLM helps the process to understand how services are performing against their targets. Incident Management also uses the targets from SLAs to help prioritise incidents and carry out impact assessment.

 Process activities

The core activities for Service Level Management relate to the agreement of targets and then managing and monitoring the agreed levels of service.

Service Level Management ensures that service reports are produced on time and distributed to the correct audience. The process will also manage any complaints or customer escalations related to services, and conduct regular service review meetings with the customer.

The service level manager is responsible for owning the service relationship with the customer. They are also responsible for discussing service level reports with them that show whether services have met their targets.

Service Level Management also provides various templates and standards, such as draft SLAs. They will provide input into the drafting of service level targets for new or radically changed services.

Service Level Management will also organise regular service review meetings. Service reviews are attended by the service level manager and customer representatives. They are held regularly – often on a monthly basis – but this is not necessarily a fixed frequency. Reviews can take place weekly, or even quarterly, depending on what is appropriate.

It is common for service reviews to be more frequent for new services, particularly if the performance is volatile, or doesn't fully meet customer requirements. Once performance settles down, the meetings can be held less frequently.

Service performance is always discussed at service reviews, as well as any changes that the customer may need.

Service reviews are an important forum for communication between the service provider and customer. It is good practice to ensure that regular communication channels are established and maintained. Customer concerns and outputs from the service review will feed into the overall Service Improvement Plan (SIP). A SIP is used to document possible improvement actions for individual services, including:

- service description
- stakeholders
- description of initiative
- business case or required impact of initiative
- impact/urgency

- status (such as approved, on hold, etc.).

Service Level Management is responsible for instigating and managing the Service Improvement Plan. It will need to interface with the CSI Register owned and operated by Continual Service Improvement.

Service Level Management will need to work closely with other areas of the service lifecycle, such as Service Operation, which provides measurement of live services, and Continual Service Improvement, which also works with the Service Improvement Plan.

 Process considerations

Service Level Management isn't something that an organisation can implement as a project and then forget about. SLAs need to be reviewed and kept up to date as the organisation grows and services change. Many organisations hire consultants to help them implement SLM, because this gives them access to the consultant's skills and templates. Once the consultants leave site, the documents are dropped into a cupboard, or file store, and not referenced again. Implementing successful Service Level Management means putting the process in place to manage the agreements, not just creating documents.

It is also tempting to create huge SLAs that are complex, wordy and cover every eventuality – don't! Start simple, more information can be added later if needed.

SLAs need to represent consensus between the business and IT. If one side doesn't engage with the process, it will fail. For example, in some organisations customers try to implement SLAs to control a service provider they perceive to be failing, but the service provider may simply ignore the targets.

Finally, be clear about what the process is trying to achieve. Some service providers will adopt an 'easy' set of targets that they know they can deliver, even if failures occur. They are frightened that if they fail a target, they will be punished. Accept that targets will be breached – but this is an opportunity for improvement, not to have a fight.

 ## Service Design process: Service Catalogue Management

The Service Catalogue is the part of the Service Portfolio that provides a view of live services, and those that are about to go live. It is visible to customers, unlike the service pipeline which is normally hidden.

A Service Catalogue can be a complex document, used by a number of different audiences, for example wholesale and retail customers. The catalogue should contain a list of all services, including a brief description. Ideally, the Service Catalogue should be in place before SLAs are documented. It is difficult to create SLAs without a comprehensive list of the services on offer.

 ## *Purpose and objectives*

The purpose of Service Catalogue Management is to provide and maintain a single source of consistent information on all operational services, and those that are about to become operational.

The Service Catalogue needs to be easily available to anyone who needs it. For example, it could be hosted on the intranet.

The process objectives include being able to:

- manage the information in the Service Catalogue
- make sure the Service Catalogue is accurate
- make sure the Service Catalogue is available and useful
- make sure the Service Catalogue supports other service management processes.

If an organisation doesn't have a Service Catalogue, it is challenging for users to understand what services are available to them.

 Scope

Services in the Service Catalogue might be listed individually, or as a set of service packages. Service packages are collections of services and Service Level Agreements that customers can choose to meet their needs – rather than having to pick lots and lots of individual services or service components. As part of its scope, Service Catalogue Management will help to define these packages.

The process will also make sure that 'service' is defined. Defining what exactly we mean by 'a service' is harder than it sounds. IT and the business will need to work together to get an agreed list of services that customers will find meaningful when they use the Service Catalogue. Technical services (such as running regular back-ups and being able to restore data) that the business might not be concerned with individually, can be classed as supporting services and hidden from the customer view, or bundled into a customer-facing service.

Service Catalogue Management will help to define the interfaces between services and service components that are recorded in the Configuration Management System and reflected in the Service Catalogue.

There are some areas specifically excluded from the scope of the process:

- capturing detailed information about service assets and configuration items (this is done by the Service Transition process of Service Asset and Configuration Management)
- recording and fulfilment of service requests for access to services (this is done by the Service Operation process of Request Fulfilment).

 Value

The Service Catalogue provides value to IT and the business. Service providers have a clearer understanding of what they offer to their customers, and how customer-facing services connect to supporting services.

All service management processes will use information from the Service Catalogue. For example, Incident Management may use the catalogue to identify what customer-facing services are affected when a supporting service fails.

The business benefits by getting a clearer view of what services are available to them. In many organisations money is wasted commissioning new services, because one part of the business did not realise the service they need already exists elsewhere in the same organisation.

 ### *Concept: Service Catalogue structure*

The structure of the Service Catalogue is important. If it is structured correctly, customers will be able to order what they need and won't be confused by too much technical information.

If the structure is set up incorrectly, customers may be confused and might even stop using the catalogue altogether.

Figure 19, overleaf, shows a two-view Service Catalogue.

The business (or customer) view shows the services that are relevant to customers, along with any links to business units, or business processes.

The technical (or supporting) view shows the supporting IT services that customers would be unlikely to order on their own. The links to the customer-facing services that they support help to show how critical a supporting service is.

Figure 20 shows a three-view Service Catalogue.

The customers have been divided into wholesale and retail categories. This allows different types of customer to be shown the information that they need, without seeing anything irrelevant.

There is no right or wrong way to structure a Service Catalogue, and each organisation will need to create a structure that works for them. The structure may well evolve as the organisational strategy evolves and customers and markets change.

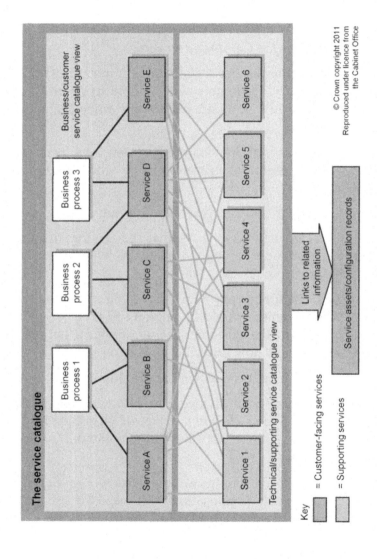

Figure 19: A two-view Service Catalogue

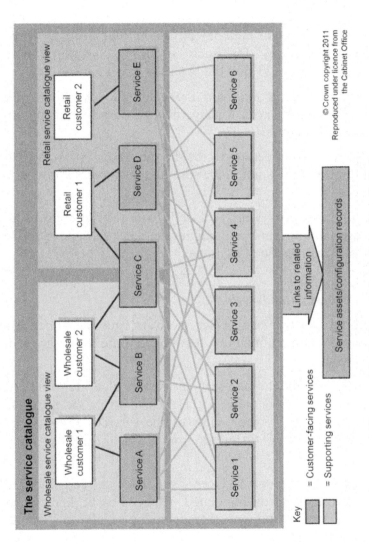

Figure 20: A three-view Service Catalogue

© Crown copyright 2011
Reproduced under licence from
the Cabinet Office

Process activities

The Service Catalogue Management process activities support its purpose and objectives. It will need to agree service definitions for each service – working with stakeholders from IT and the business to get a clear picture.

It will create and maintain the catalogue, working with other teams and service management processes to keep it up to date and accurate.

The process will need to decide the most appropriate way to host the catalogue, and make sure that customers know how to access it.

The process also works closely with Service Portfolio Management to maintain alignment between the Service Portfolio and Service Catalogue.

 ### *Process considerations*

It is hard to implement a Service Catalogue, and once it's been implemented, it can be hard to keep the information in it up to date.

Process implementation must start with a clear definition of what a 'service' actually is. IT must consult the business during this stage – their view of the services IT provides may be radically different from what IT thinks they provide.

Once the high-level services have been agreed and the Service Catalogue is populated, it needs to be kept up to date. Service Catalogue Management needs to link to processes including Change Management and Service Portfolio Management to help it do this. If these processes are not in place, then Service Catalogue Management will have to work much harder to keep track of service changes and updates.

Don't rush straight in and buy an expensive toolset as part of the process implementation. Service Catalogues often start as a simple spreadsheet or matrix, before evolving to views that are more complex. It's the information in the catalogue and its accessibility that's important – not the fanciness of the tool used to support it.

Service Design process: Availability Management

Availability Management is a service management process that extends right across the service lifecycle, but its most critical responsibility is during Service Design activities.

Availability Management makes sure the availability requirements of the business are understood, and are designed into each new or changed service. This means that services match the needs of the business and are delivered cost effectively.

The latest trends in technology, and business reliance on IT, mean that availability is becoming more and more important. For example, end-users of IT services expect their services to be available for longer periods of time to suit their working patterns, as well as being made available from more places – to suit mobile and home working.

Availability Management needs to consider these requirements whilst the service is being designed. It's much more expensive to correct a service after it goes live, if the availability requirements are not being met. Changes to live services can also mean disruption for the business, affecting service performance and the reputation of the service provider.

 Purpose and objectives

The purpose of Availability Management is to make sure that the level of service availability delivered for an IT service meets the agreed targets. This has to be done in a cost-effective and timely manner.

As well as current business needs, Availability Management needs to consider future business needs and how they may change.

As part of its objectives, Availability Management will produce an Availability Plan that documents the current and future business needs, based on possible scenarios. This could include what would happen if the business grew, stayed the same or contracted in the next financial period. The plan is normally updated annually, and shows where investment is needed to continue to meet availability targets.

Availability Management will also advise the business and other IT teams on any availability issues.

The process will monitor services to make sure availability targets are met, and help with any availability incidents, or problems such as service downtime. Availability Management will also interface with Change Management and provide input into decisions about whether changes are likely to affect service availability. They will identify any possible proactive measures to improve availability, and implement them where cost-justified.

Effective monitoring is essential for the Availability Management process to be able to fulfil its role.

 Scope

Availability Management process activity starts when the availability requirements for an IT service are clear, and doesn't finish until a service is retired. It includes the design, implementation, measurement, management, and improvement of IT service and component availability.

The process has two key elements:

- **Reactive activities:** that deal with operational issues, such as incidents and problems.
- **Proactive activities:** that plan for improvement and make sure availability is designed into services.

To carry out its role effectively, Availability Management must understand business and IT information. They need to be aware of business requirements, and also how technology can be exploited to deliver business outcomes.

Availability Management should be applied to all services, planned and live. Its scope will also extend to third-party elements of services. For these, it will have a governance and management role, rather than a practical hands-on role.

One area that is explicitly out of scope for Availability Management is the restoration of service after a period of severe disruption – such as a fire or power outage. This falls within the scope of IT Service Continuity Management.

The availability manager will work with any customer requirements that have been fed into Service Design. The role is also responsible for measuring availability and producing reports at both the service and component levels.

The process activities should include:

- monitoring IT services to track availability
- producing availability reports, including agreed metrics and calculations for components and end-to-end service availability
- carrying out risk management related to availability
- carrying out testing of fail-over and resilience arrangements.

 Value

Availability Management is essential to make sure that IT services stay aligned with business needs. Levels of availability that were acceptable last year may not be acceptable this year. As businesses evolve, their availability requirements will change – typically wanting more availability, not less.

Availability Management is extremely closely linked to customer satisfaction. If a service is down, it doesn't matter how great its functionality is, because it can't be accessed. Customers who experience consistently poor service availability are very likely to change service provider. They will look for someone who can guarantee the availability they need.

 Concept: service and component level monitoring

Availability Management needs to measure service components and technology, and then build up a view of end-to-end service availability. By measuring at service and component levels, the availability manager will produce reports that are relevant to customers and the technical teams within the service provider.

Customers typically want to see end-to-end measures of service availability. This could be given as a percentage, for example, the e-mail service was available 98.9% of the time during the last reporting period. If e-mail was not available for some reason, remember that the customer is not necessarily interested in which actual component failed and caused the downtime.

Availability monitoring also looks at individual configuration items, such as servers, network links and routers. This level of monitoring is far more relevant to the service provider, as it needs to understand the real impact of any component failure on the overall service, and see where the infrastructure could be improved.

If a service needs to be highly available, then component resilience will be built in – for example, duplicate network links or mirrored servers. This means that if a component fails, the overall service availability is not affected.

Component availability can have an impact on service availability, so it's important for Availability Management to work at these two interconnected levels.

All aspects of service and component availability and unavailability need to be understood. The definitions are:

*'**Service availability:** involves all aspects of service availability and unavailability and the impact of component availability, or unavailability on service availability.'*

*'**Component availability:** involves all aspects of component availability and unavailability.'*

Concept: availability measures

The table below defines some of the main availability terminology.

Availability
'Availability is the ability of an IT service or other configuration item to perform its agreed function when required.' Availability is defined as a service or IT component being 'up' or available when needed. Modern technology can deliver high availability services, and customers will not be happy with poor availability. Availability is normally measured during agreed service time (AST). Downtime outside the normal service hours still needs to be monitored, but will not have the same impact on the user. The higher the availability required for a service, the greater the cost of providing it. This is why it's so important to collect accurate availability requirements during the design stage. The more redundancy and duplication in the infrastructure, the higher the service cost and the more components involved with its delivery. Availability is often reported as a percentage, but this can be difficult for customers to understand. Other measures, for example, minutes of downtime, can better reflect the customer experience.
Reliability
'Reliability is a measure of how long an IT service or other configuration item can perform its agreed function without interruption.' This is a measure of how frequently a service or component is unavailable. The more infrequently the service or component breaks down, the more reliable it is.

Customers expect IT services to be reliable, just like an automobile, or household appliance. Reliability is often measured as the mean time between failures (MTBF).

Maintainability
'Maintainability is a measure of how quickly and effectively an IT service or other configuration item can be restored to normal working after a failure.' This is a measure of how easy it is to restore the service back to working order, once it has broken down. If a service takes a week to get back up and running each time it breaks down, this might not be a satisfactory level of maintainability. This is measured as mean time to restore service (MTRS).

Serviceability
'Serviceability is the ability of a third-party supplier to meet the terms of its contract. This contract will include agreed levels of reliability, availability and maintainability for a configuration item.' This means that the availability, reliability or maintainability have been contracted out to a third party – who will manage these specific levels on our behalf.

Table 10: Availability terminology

 Concept: vital business function

A vital business function (VBF) defines the critical part of a business service.

For example, the finance department might run a payroll process. The process calculates the correct amount to pay staff, transfers money and provides historical reports on payments made.

Paying staff is a VBF. Without pay, staff might refuse to work. Providing reports could be seen as less critical, because the business can survive for a period of time without this information.

From a service management perspective, resources would be targeted towards the service assets that support the VBF. It's not efficient to offer the same level of availability and protection for the whole business process, so time and resources need to be carefully targeted.

 Process activities: Reactive Availability Management

Reactive Availability Management measures and monitors services and components to check if the level of availability delivered matches the business requirements.

Common reports will include:

- percentage availability
- percentage unavailability
- duration of downtime
- frequency of failure
- impact of failure.

To be effective, Availability Management needs data and information to show it where improvements need to be made.

There are a number of techniques used by Availability Management as part of its reactive activities. These are detailed in Table 11, overleaf.

Unavailability analysis

This technique investigates incidents or events that have affected availability.

It includes examination of records and logs to find evidence of unavailability, and then calculates the impact of the loss of availability. Impact can include tangible factors (such as loss of staff productivity in IT and the business) and intangible factors (such as loss of goodwill or reputational damage).

The expanded incident lifecycle

This technique breaks down the lifecycle of an incident to identify where improvements could potentially be made. Each incident includes detection, diagnosis, repair, recovery and restoration before closure.

Analysis may show, for example, that repair is taking a large percentage of the duration of an incident. This could highlight a number of improvement areas, such as staff training for technical teams, or replacing ageing hardware that is becoming harder to fix.

Service failure analysis (SFA)

This technique tries to identify the underlying causes of unavailability, and is often carried out in conjunction with Problem Management.

Groups of incidents or events will feed into the analysis, and IT and the business will both contribute to the process.

The steps in a service failure analysis include:

- Selecting the opportunity – which service or technology will be assessed?

- Scoping the assignment – what will and will not be covered?

- Planning the assignment – what inputs are needed? Who will be involved?

- Building hypotheses – what scenarios can be used to prompt discussion?

- Analysing data – some early conclusions may be drawn here.

- Interviewing key personnel – whose input is vital? Is anyone missing or not available?

- Findings and conclusions – based on the analysis.

- Recommendations – what can be improved?

- Reporting – information needs to be presented in the right format to the right audience.

- Validation – it's essential to use measures to check the SFA really did deliver improvements.

Table 11: Reactive Availability Management techniques

 Process activities: Proactive Availability Management

Proactive Availability Management tries to reduce the likelihood of a loss of availability by making sure that services are designed properly and then monitoring and analysing them to identify any risks.

Table 12, which follows, shows some of the proactive Availability Management techniques.

Designing availability

One of the best ways to get service availability right is to design services properly in the first place. This will include collecting accurate business requirements and getting them signed off by the business, and identifying the vital business functions supported by the process, which need to be protected. Using this information, Availability Management will work with other design processes to deliver the right service, first time.

Remember, service availability is not just about technology. The processes, people and suppliers involved in service delivery will all have an impact on availability.

Component failure impact analysis (CFIA)

This technique analyses an organisation's infrastructure to try to predict what will happen if a component or service becomes unavailable. For example, if a router fails, what is the impact on the network? How many users or services are affected?

This technique is used to highlight critical or overloaded services and components, which may need more protection because they are so important.

This technique relies on an accurate view of what our infrastructure looks like – without accurate input information, the results of the analysis are likely to be incorrect.

Single point of failure analysis (SPOF)

Single points of failure can be technology, people or processes. When they fail, they cause an effect because they have no redundancy or countermeasures in place.

Component failure impact analysis will often identify SPOFs. SPOFs should be recorded and assessed. Countermeasures can then be applied to eliminate the SPOF, if it is justified by the service criticality or business need.

Fault tree analysis (FTA)

This technique looks at the chain of events that might affect a service's availability. For example, either a server or a network failure could result in a service being down – but only if they happen inside service hours. Boolean notation is applied to create a diagram showing the possible fault tree.

Availability Management will analyse the output from the FTA to identify areas where improvements or countermeasures would be cost-justified.

Modelling

Modelling tools can be used to forecast what might happen if demand changes, or new or changed services are introduced.

Simulation, modelling and load-testing tools can all be used to give an accurate view of future availability and service performance. Simple calculations using spreadsheets or existing data can also give a reasonable level of accuracy.

The amount of money invested in modelling will be influenced by the impact to the business of any availability deterioration.

Risk assessment and management

Availability Management, IT Service Continuity Management and Information Security Management all carry out risk assessment and management.

Availability Management will be particularly interested in any risks that may lead to a loss of availability at a service or component level.

There are many risk management methodologies available – check to see what already exists in your organisation and if there is anything you can use.

Implementation of countermeasures
Based on the analysis techniques, Availability Management will identify countermeasures or improvements that can improve availability, or remove risk.
These must only be implemented if they are cost-justified. Remember, every company in the world can potentially deliver 100% availability for every service – but the costs would be astronomical.
Business cases must be used to assess whether money should be spent or not.
Continual review and improvement
Finally (and it sounds obvious) Availability Management needs to keep going.
A service might be performing brilliantly today, but that doesn't mean it will be okay next week. All of the proactive activities need to be carried out constantly, so that improvements can be identified, recorded and acted on where justified.

Table 12: Proactive Availability Management techniques

 Process considerations

Many organisations have tried to make the business case for Availability Management, only to have the management team tell them 'things are fine! Why should we spend any money?'

It is important to understand that just because things are okay today, it doesn't mean they'll be okay tomorrow. Sadly, the aftermath of a major incident, or availability loss, can be a great time to get some funding and management attention for the implementation of Availability Management.

The actual definition of availability can also be tough. Services that are 'up' or 'down' are easy to identify, but what about intermittent availability, or degraded performance? Does that mean the service is available or not? The service provider and the customer might have very different views here. Service Level Management and Business Relationship Management can help Availability Management to talk to the customer and get a precise definition for service up and service down.

Finally, remember that Availability Management is a complex, technical process. The process won't normally work closely with customers, apart from when it's carrying out analysis and impact assessment. Be very wary of customers who have heard figures they like the sound of (for example 99.999% or '5 9s') and ask for that as an availability target.

It's sensible to check that the customer knows exactly what they are asking for and why – and if they are prepared to pay for the service. It's a good idea to draw up a table to show your customer exactly what these figures mean in terms of minutes of downtime per week, month or year.

 Service Design process: Information Security Management

Information Security Management is responsible for aligning IT security with the business security policy and making sure that effective levels of security are designed into all new services and service management activities.

Any security policies in place need to align with the overall corporate governance framework.

An organisation can build the best new service in the world, but if it's not secure people will not be prepared to use it. Imagine if you thought your internet banking was not secure. Would you use it?

Information Security Management sets standards that need to be available to everyone in the business. The standards should cover areas such as acceptable usage of e-mail and web browsing standards.

Security is part of the **warranty** of a service.

 Purpose and objectives

Information Security Management aligns IT security with business security requirements, protecting the organisation's assets, data and information. The process is concerned with confidentiality and integrity, and restricting availability to those who have a right to access services and information.

The process objectives relate to the protection of information and the people who use information.

The impact of a security breach can be huge. It could include losses, fines, or customers moving to another supplier with a better reputation for security.

The security objective is met when information:

- **is confidential:** it is only accessed by those who have the right to see it
- **has integrity:** it is complete, accurate and protected from unapproved change

- **is available and usable when needed:** information can resist and recover from attacks or failures
- **has authenticity and non-repudiation:** information shared between organisations or partners can be trusted.

 Scope

The scope of Information Security Management includes being a focal point for all security issues.

The process will produce a policy that outlines the organisational approach to security. This will be linked to any overall business security plans and policies, as well as any legislative requirements.

Security issues need to be prioritised according to the overall business goals and priorities.

The information security policy should be available to everyone. IT staff will need access to it and users will need to understand their obligations. In some organisations, the policy will also need to be available to third-party staff – such as maintenance staff working on site.

The security policy sets out standards for many areas, including the use of passwords, e-mail and internet browsing. Adequate levels of security should be designed into each new service and the information security policy will be updated if required. The security policy covers everything that could have a potential impact on security – anti-virus, information classification, remote access, copyright, asset disposal, access control, passwords, etc.

The information security manager is responsible for ensuring that all security policies are communicated, fully implemented and enforced. The policies need to be integrated at all levels of the organisation: strategic, tactical and operational.

Every single user has the potential to cause a security breach, so training and communication is critical. For example, security inductions for new starters might include not sharing their password, or leaving their desk without locking their PC.

Another responsibility of the Information Security Management process is to manage any security breaches, for example, virus outbreaks or unauthorised access to a system.

Security breaches will need to be prioritised and appropriate action must be taken to resolve the breach. There will be a review after the breach to see if any lessons need to be learned, or processes updated.

Information Security Management also organises regular security reviews and security tests. These reviews and tests will all help to ensure that the policies and measures put in place are performing as they should.

 Value

An effective Information Security Management process protects the IT services and information that are the lifeblood of the business. The impact of a security breach does not just affect IT – it affects the business, its reputation and its business processes.

An effective security management process will give customers the confidence that they are protected when using services. This will help to reinforce the strong relationship between customer and service provider.

Customers are becoming more and more educated about IT services and security. For example, many customers will check for the 'https:' that signifies a secure webpage. They would not enter their financial information onto a page they thought was insecure.

 Concept: Information Security Management System (ISMS)

Figure 21, below shows an Information Security Management System, used by Information Security Management to establish a policy and objectives, and ensure objectives are met.

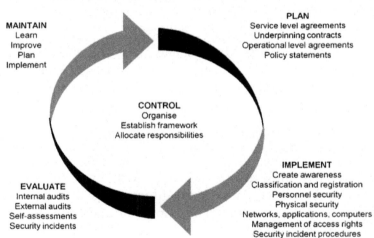

Customers – requirements – business needs

MAINTAIN
Learn
Improve
Plan
Implement

PLAN
Service level agreements
Underpinning contracts
Operational level agreements
Policy statements

CONTROL
Organise
Establish framework
Allocate responsibilities

IMPLEMENT
Create awareness
Classification and registration
Personnel security
Physical security
Networks, applications, computers
Management of access rights
Security incident procedures

EVALUATE
Internal audits
External audits
Self-assessments
Security incidents

Figure 21: Elements of an ISMS for managing IT security

Control

This element puts a management framework in place. It also defines the required responsibilities and supporting documentation.

Plan

This element recommends security measures aligned to organisational needs. The type of organisation using the IT services and the market they operate in will affect the level of security that needs to be in place.

Implement

This element puts the underpinning procedures, tools and controls in place. This will include carrying out education and awareness, and using management support to cascade information from the security policy to operational teams.

Evaluate

This element monitors and audits compliance with security policies and procedures. This might include internal and external audits – depending on the policy in place.

Maintain

This element supports gradual improvement and aligns the system with changing business requirements as IT services and processes change and evolve.

Process activities

The Information Security Management process focuses on the implementation of appropriate security measures, aligned with organisational requirements. They will monitor for compliance, and manage any breaches that occur.

Different security measures will be put in place to protect different categories of information:

- **Preventive**: these measures prevent a security incident occurring. For example, restricting the users who access a service will help to prevent unauthorised activity.
- **Reductive**: these are measures taken in advance to minimise the impact of an incident. This could include backing up data so that it can be restored easily.
- **Detective**: these measures discover when an incident has occurred. Network monitoring might, for example, detect unusual volumes of traffic that indicate a virus.
- **Repressive**: these measures prevent the incident continuing or being repeated. For example, an infected machine might be removed from the network and placed into quarantine to stop a virus spreading.
- **Corrective**: these measures repair the damage where possible. This could include running anti-virus software to remove any unauthorised programs, and restoring data to an earlier version that has not been corrupted.

 ## Process considerations

Many service management processes are implemented in silos, and security management is no exception. It's common for someone to be put 'in charge' of security and then left to try to get on with it. Without management support, they feel like they are pushing water uphill trying to get other staff to follow the policies and procedures they are implementing.

Management backing is essential for this process. Staff will have to change their behaviour and they may resist this. It can be hard to achieve cultural change with a bottom-up implementation – some top-down direction and support from management is needed.

Remember where this process sits in the service lifecycle. Considering security at the design stage can be extremely helpful. If a service goes live with security measures built in, there will be less manual work to do later in the lifecycle.

A lot of security management is automated. Access to services, audit trails, etc. all support this process. We should not, however, rely on automation alone to implement security management – the biggest danger to any organisation is usually the person sitting at the desk.

 Service Design process: Supplier Management

Supplier Management is responsible for getting the right suppliers and the right contracts in place for an organisation. Their expertise is invaluable and protects the business from unclear, inaccurate or poorly thought out agreements.

 Purpose and objectives

Supplier Management is responsible for managing suppliers and the services that they supply, to provide a seamless quality of IT service to the business, ensuring value for money is obtained.

The process is responsible for managing the full lifecycle of a supplier relationship. This starts by identifying a need, choosing the supplier and making sure the correct contract is in place, and carrying out any necessary negotiation.

Once the supplier has been chosen and the contract is in place, they will be monitored on an ongoing basis, in line with the organisation's overall supplier policy. At the end of the contract, the termination or renegotiation process also needs to be managed.

Most organisations will have a number of different suppliers. Some suppliers will provide business critical services and products, whilst others will provide less important services and products. The least critical suppliers are usually those who provide your organisation with consumables – for example, printer toner cartridges.

 Scope

Supplier Management includes all suppliers and contracts related to IT services. If an organisation has inherited any old contracts that aren't really fit for purpose, Supplier Management will try to improve them, or optimise them until they expire.

To help manage suppliers, the process will implement a supplier policy outlining who the organisation will do business with, when, and how.

The process will maintain supplier records in a Supplier and Contract Management Information System (SCMIS), and work proactively through the whole contract lifecycle.

Value

Many organisations unknowingly waste money on duplicate contracts, or trying to manage suppliers who just don't do the job. An effective Supplier Management process centralises the control of supplier-related activity, giving a clear picture of who the organisation has agreements with, what for, and when the agreements expire.

The business should not have to worry about which suppliers are providing part or all of their IT services. They should have confidence that the suppliers chosen are the right ones, and that services will be provided seamlessly and cost effectively.

 Process activities

The activities of the Supplier Management process cover the full contract lifecycle, from identifying the need and choosing a supplier, through negotiation and performance management.

One of the most critical process activities is supplier categorisation. Suppliers should be categorised so that it is clear how much actual management each supplier and their corresponding contract(s) need. The more disruption the loss of any particular supplier's service would cause, the more effort that needs to be put into managing that particular relationship.

The categories suggested for suppliers are strategic, tactical, operational and commodity suppliers.

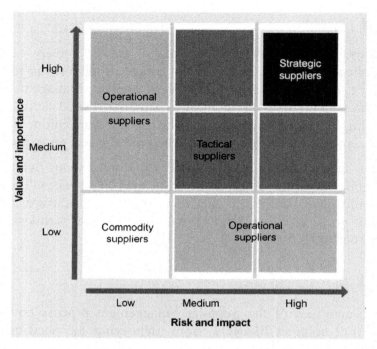

Figure 22: Supplier categorisation

- **Strategic suppliers:** these are significant partnering relationships, managed by senior managers. Confidential and strategic information is shared between the customer and the supplier, and loss of a supplier at this level could mean the business strategy was at risk of not being achieved.
- **Tactical suppliers:** these are relationships with significant commercial activity and business interaction. Tactical suppliers are normally managed by middle

management, with regular communication and performance reviews.

- **Operational suppliers:** these relationships are managed by junior management and relate to operational products and services. If the supplier is performing well, there will be infrequent communication between the parties.
- **Commodity suppliers:** this category is used for suppliers providing low-value services that are easily replaced. If a supplier under-performs here, the sourcing organisation is more likely to switch supplier than put any effort into making improvements.

Process considerations

If your organisation doesn't already have a centralised Supplier Management process, get ready to do some detective work. It's likely that individual teams and departments have been allowed to make their own agreements at the operational and commodity level, so there will be contracts everywhere.

It's essential to start with a sound Supplier Management policy. This will set staff expectations about how they need to behave when selecting a new supplier, and why. Once this is in place, the situation will start to improve.

Some customers have found themselves stuck with a supplier or a contract that was negotiated in the past and just doesn't work. It is important to try to recover the situation as far as possible, or check the cost of early termination if the relationship has irretrievably broken down.

If you're looking to enter into a contract with a supplier for all or part of service provision, be very clear about exactly what you want. Too many contracts are based on a fuzzy understanding of what's needed, with extra services added at extra cost once the initial contract is in place. Getting the right agreement in place will save time, money and heartache in the future.

Service Design process: Capacity Management

Like Availability Management, Capacity Management extends right across the service lifecycle and has activities in every phase. However, it has a crucial responsibility during Service Design to make sure the required level of capacity is designed into new or changed services.

A lack of capacity means that something has run out of space. If a server reaches maximum capacity, or an organisation runs out of network bandwidth, this can significantly affect the performance of a service.

Purpose and objectives

The purpose of Capacity Management is to make sure that the capacity of IT services and infrastructure in place meets the agreed business requirements in a cost-effective and timely manner. This involves planning ahead in order to predict the right capacity requirements for a new service. This will avoid any future suffering from downtime caused by a lack of capacity.

Capacity Management is interested in service performance. It will look at how current performance can be maintained and improved.

Capacity Management has a number of objectives. It will produce a Capacity Plan, which provides costed options to meet current and future business needs.

It will advise the business and IT about capacity-related concerns, and make sure that services are not affected by issues related to capacity.

The Capacity Management process will carry out reactive activities, working with processes such as Incident and Problem Management when service has been affected by a capacity-related issue.

It will also have a proactive role, carrying out change impact assessments and implementing any cost-justified measures that could improve service performance.

 ## Scope

The scope of Capacity Management includes being the organisation's focal point for capacity information.

The process encompasses hardware, software, infrastructure and even people. For example, if the staff on the Service Desk reach maximum capacity, no further calls can be taken. Their time needs to be planned and managed like any other service asset, and Capacity Management techniques may be applied for this.

Capacity Management needs to work closely with Service Strategy to make sure it understands and plans for long-term business needs, and doesn't just react to short-term changes. To fulfil its role, Capacity Management needs monitoring capabilities to support it. If capacity isn't monitored, there is a risk that potential problems will not be detected until service has been affected.

Capacity Management will constantly tune and refine services and infrastructure to optimise their performance.

The scope of Capacity Management also includes understanding how technology can improve services and service performance. If a service is not performing well and investment is not available to increase capacity, Capacity Management may try to influence demand instead. The process will work closely with Demand Management.

Capacity Management may also work with Financial Management when it considers measures such as peak and off-peak charging for a service.

 Value

An effective Capacity Management process improves the performance of IT services, which can in turn improve their availability.

Careful capacity planning during Service Design optimises services. Organisations want to be efficient and spend just the right amount of money on capacity and resources. They don't want to spend too much and have spare capacity, and they don't want to spend too little and not have enough.

 Concept: Capacity Management sub-processes

There are three Capacity Management sub-processes: business, service and component Capacity Management.

Business Capacity Management operates at the strategic level. It looks at how the future plans of the business might affect capacity, for example, during an expansion, merger or acquisition.

The sub-process focuses on predicting future capacity usage, based on business plans and trend analysis of current growth and usage. It helps to translate business plans and needs into requirements.

Service Capacity Management operates at the tactical level. It will review current capacity levels and changing levels of demand to make sure that capacity issues will not cause service target breaches.

The sub-process monitors day-to-day activity and service usage to provide information for trend analysis. It will work to ensure that targets in SLAs and SLRs can be monitored and achieved.

Component Capacity Management is involved with the technology that makes up the IT infrastructure. Individual IT components all need to be monitored and measured to build up a complete picture of the capacity available to deliver services.

This is the most technical sub-process. It is here that IT components will be fine-tuned and adjusted to deliver optimum capacity. The sub-process manages, controls and predicts component performance, utilisation and capacity.

All Capacity Management sub-processes rely on monitoring to provide source information. This monitoring should be automated as far as possible. If automated monitoring is not available, the sub-processes can be extremely labour-intensive and manual.

Concept: the Capacity Plan

Capacity Management will produce the Capacity Plan. This is usually produced on an annual basis, in line with the organisation's financial cycle.

The plan will include:

- current and historic use of IT services and components from a capacity perspective
- any issues or improvement activities
- scenarios for different projected levels of business demand
- the investment required to meet service targets, including costed options.

The Capacity Plan will be used by IT and the business to support overall planning activities and to help define the level of funding required for IT. Funding may be allocated to maintain existing services, or to allow expansion into new services and types of technology.

 Process activities

Capacity Management will carry out reactive and proactive activities. Proactive activities include modelling and trending to predict future performance and requirements, and taking action to try to prevent any capacity-related issues occurring.

Reactive Capacity Management activities include ongoing monitoring and measurement of services and service components, taking action whenever any issues are identified. Capacity Management will work closely with Incident and Problem Management here.

Process considerations

Capacity Management is about more than just technology – it is about putting policies and procedures in place to govern capacity.

Business users do not always respond well to requests for more capacity investment (or to being asked to use less capacity). Home computing and the falling price of storage media both contribute to a 'just buy more space' attitude from the business. When implementing Capacity Management, it's important to educate the business about the cost of capacity. This isn't just the purchase price of storage, it's the ongoing costs of housing, maintaining and backing-up the data stored on it.

The information being stored by the business should be classified and sensible retention policies can be put into place. Data can also be archived if it isn't regularly used, with access available on request.

Investment in capacity should be made 'just in time'. This means that capacity is bought when needed – it doesn't mean that it's bought at the last minute! If an organisation buys capacity too soon, it risks having idle space. A delay in investment might benefit the organisation if the cost of technology falls significantly. If an organisation buys capacity too late, the performance of a service might have already been affected.

 Service Design process: IT Service Continuity Management

IT Service Continuity Management (ITSCM) deals with situations that could have a severe effect on the business, such as a fire, power outage, major incident or flood. This is often referred to as disaster recovery planning.

ITSCM is applied to business critical services. It includes planning to protect them from significant disruption, and also planning how to successfully recover from service loss if disruption occurs.

 Purpose and objectives

The purpose of ITSCM is to support the overall Business Continuity Management process by making sure that minimum agreed levels of services can be delivered in a highly disruptive situation. This is done by managing the risk to services, and planning for service recovery when required.

One of the important points to be aware of when implementing ITSCM is that it has to be integrated with the organisational Business Continuity Plans. This means that IT should never be acting alone when developing the IT Service Continuity Plan.

It is not within the scope of the service provider to decide how long the business can cope without any particular service, or which service is the most important. Instead, Business Continuity Management (BCM) should provide this information to IT Service Continuity Management.

The objectives of ITSCM include:

• Maintaining the IT Service Continuity Plans and IT recovery plans. The plans need to be updated and regularly assessed to make sure they still support the Business Continuity Plans.

- Carrying out regular Business Impact Analysis exercises, to make sure that the changing criticality of business services is reflected in the plans.
- Carrying out risk analysis and management, and providing advice and guidance as needed.
- Assessing the impact of all changes on the plans.
- Negotiating contracts with any suppliers who provide services that support the plans.

📋 *Scope*

The scope of ITSCM is whatever the business deems to be a significantly disruptive situation. Less significant downtime will be managed by processes such as Incident Management.

ITSCM planning is harder for more complex services. Simple services may have a relatively simple plan, but services that span multiple locations and involve third-party suppliers will require plans that are more detailed.

One area that is out of scope for ITSCM is long-term business changes that could affect the organisation. For example, a major restructure could significantly affect services, but this would not be managed by ITSCM. These events need to be planned for at the business level, as part of the organisation's overall strategic planning.

As part of its scope, ITSCM follows a four step process:

- **Initiation**: this is where ITSCM begins, driven by Business Continuity Management.
- **Requirements and strategy:** this step includes carrying out Business Impact Analysis and risk assessment to identify critical services.

- **Implementation**: this includes production of plans and implementation of risk reduction measures.
- **Ongoing operation**: includes operational management and updates, as well as regular testing of the plans.

 Value

Although ITSCM should be driven by the business, in many organisations the reverse is actually true. In these organisations, ITSCM is used to raise awareness of continuity requirements and planning, leading to improvements for IT and the business.

Implementing an ITSCM process can clarify requirements for Business Continuity Management and lead to positive changes in the business, as well as the IT service provider. An effective ITSCM process will lead to improved customer confidence that services can continue to be provided, no matter what happens. Global events, such as riots, terrorist activity and power failures, have all raised user awareness of the need for continuity planning.

 Concept: Business Impact Analysis (BIA)

One of the techniques used by ITSCM is Business Impact Analysis. This is a way of determining the effect to the business of service loss. This can be financial – such as a fine – or non-financial – such as loss of goodwill. Tangible impacts are easy to measure and quantify. Intangible impacts, such as a damaged reputation, are much harder to quantify.

The output from a Business Impact Analysis exercise is usually a graph, which shows how the effect can escalate over time. This can be used to identify the minimum amount of staff and infrastructure required to maintain service.

Business Impact Analysis can help to guide ITSCM efforts and investment. It also helps to determine recovery requirements and recovery times.

 Concept: risk assessment

ITSCM uses risk assessment to help identify what to protect and how much to invest in protective measures. Risk assessment is also used by Availability Management and Information Security Management when they are protecting services.

Standard methodologies like Management of Risk (MoR®) can be used to create a profile of risk. The risks that have the highest chance of materialising or affecting a business critical service may require countermeasures to reduce their likelihood.

Risk assessment helps to determine risk responses and risk reduction, based on a risk profile.

 Process activities

Process stage 1: initiation

During this process stage, the overall ITSCM policy is set and communicated to all relevant stakeholders. It is important to start with a clear understanding of what is being done and why. The scope and terms of reference for the process will be defined, and a project initiated.

The nature of ITSCM planning (collecting requirements, carrying out planning activities, producing deliverables, etc.) is very similar to a project, so it's helpful to use any existing project management methodology within the organisation.

Using a project management methodology means that resources can be allocated and managed, with an appropriate control structure and quality plan tracking the deliverables.

Process stage 2: requirements and strategy

During the requirements stage, the Business Impact Analysis and risk assessment techniques are used. The output from these exercises will dictate the strategy for risk reduction measures and recovery options.

It's important to note that ITSCM will take action in two main areas:

- **Risk response:** countermeasures or risk reduction activities reduce the likelihood of service disruption.
- **Recovery options:** plans are put in place for when disruption does happen.

It is not usually cost-justifiable to remove every single risk from the IT infrastructure.

Table 13 shows some of the common ITSCM recovery options.

Manual workaround	Manual workarounds can be used to replace the IT service – for example, customer orders might be recorded on paper forms, instead of using the IT service.
	This option will normally only work for a short time, and needs to include a plan for rekeying data back into the system, once it has been recovered.
Reciprocal arrangement	No longer common, this arrangement allowed two similar organisations to support each other. For example, utilities providers could offer to print each other's bills in the event of one organisation losing their printing facilities.
	Competition and data security considerations and the increasing complexity of IT systems have made this arrangement less practical.
	It is still used in the public sector, and may be used by public and private organisations for less complex measures like off-site storage of back-ups.
Gradual recovery	Sometimes referred to as cold standby, this option provides empty accommodation with power, network and communications connections.
	In the event of a disaster, computing equipment has to be procured or shipped to the location, so this won't be suitable for a service that needs very quick recovery.
	Gradual recovery premises can be maintained by the organisation itself, or leased from a third party. They can also be fixed (a building) or portable (a mobile building or even a truck).

Intermediate recovery	This option is sometimes referred to as warm standby. It includes a site with computer equipment, but the organisation's services may need to be installed.
	This option will be suitable for services with a defined recovery time (e.g. within 36 hours), and can also be provided internally or externally by a third party.
Fast recovery	This option is sometimes referred to as hot standby. It offers accommodation, computer equipment with services installed, so the only delay is while customers are switched over and the very latest data is restored.
	This is suitable for services that require a 24-hour or less recovery period.
Immediate recovery	This option is also referred to as hot standby, mirroring, load balancing or split site. Services can be restored immediately, with very little customer impact.
	This is suitable for the most critical IT services and requires dual-located equipment.

Table 13: ITSCM recovery options

Most organisations will adopt a mixture of recovery options, spending more money on faster recovery options for critical services and vital business functions. The faster the recovery required, the higher the cost of providing the recovery option.

Process stage 3: implementation

During this stage, the IT Service Continuity Plans and procedures will be developed. The actions needed, the chain of command, and roles and responsibilities during a period of significant disruption all need documenting and agreeing. Any agreed risk reduction measures will be put in place at this point.

During implementation, initial testing is also carried out. This is different to ongoing operational tests, and is basically a sense check to ensure that nothing has been missed.

Before 'live' tests using real systems are scheduled, it's a good idea to do some simulated or paper-based tests – these will highlight any major omissions in the plan.

Process stage 4: ongoing operation

Once plans are in place, they need to be kept up to date. IT systems and environments change constantly, and it may be too late when you realise the plan is no longer valid.

This stage includes:

- education, awareness and training to keep staff abreast of their role
- review and audit to make sure the plans are current
- testing following changes, and regular testing
- integration with the Change Management process.

Process activities: invocation

As well as planning for recovery from service disruption, organisations need to protect themselves by making sure the ITSC plan isn't invoked incorrectly.

If external service providers are being used for recovery facilities, there will usually be a cost for invoking the plan and using their services. Invocation planning needs to state clearly who is allowed to invoke the plan, and under what circumstances.

Process activities: return to normal working

Following invocation of the ITSC plan, the business should be able to access services at an agreed level. This doesn't, however, mean the role of ITSCM is complete. The process needs to focus on building the business back to normal levels and vacating the recovery site as quickly as possible.

These activities are classed as 'return to normal working'. The goal is to get the business back to the state it was in before the disruption occurred. It can be very expensive to operate services from a recovery site, and services may be provided at lower levels than normal.

The ITSC plan must address how the business will return to its former state.

 Process considerations

ITSCM is another service management process that often starts with a blaze of glory. Ironically, the best time to get funding to start this process is directly after a period of extreme disruption, when the business realises what it has to lose and why it needs to plan.

In the initial excitement, consultants will be hired and documents drawn up ... but organisations also need to plan for what happens when the consultants leave site.

Has a process owner been put in place? Is there a genuine commitment to the process? Will ongoing testing be seen as a priority, or gradually dropped in favour of the day job?

The level of commitment to ITSCM will always be linked to the type of organisation and the markets it operates in. If the organisation operates in a risk averse, time critical, heavily regulated market it is much more likely to invest in ITSCM. Imagine a bank having a service loss and saying 'sorry, we can't recover your information'.

ITSCM also tends to become more of a concern as organisations mature. Immature organisations are usually much more focused on day-to-day activities and just hope things won't happen. Mature organisations will consider the risks more carefully and start to plan for when things go wrong.

 Service Design process: Design Coordination

Design Coordination provides a focal point for all Service Design processes and activities, and makes sure that design goals are met.

Without good coordination, there is a risk that all the other Service Design processes will work in isolation, leading to poor quality services and failed designs that do not integrate well.

Purpose and objectives

To fulfil its purpose, Design Coordination needs to make sure that all the design processes work consistently. It will coordinate resources and make sure plans are handed over to Service Transition in a timely way. The process is responsible for the production of the Service Design Package, which is the output of Service Design, handed to Service Transition.

It will also make sure that all service designs conform to any overall corporate requirements. The Design Coordination process improves overall Service Design effectiveness and efficiency. It provides a common framework of standard, reusable practices, and identifies improvements that can be made.

 Scope

The scope of Design Coordination covers all design activities, no matter what the technology or service involved. The more complex the design, the more coordination is needed. Each organisation will need to have guidelines to make sure that each design, or project, gets an appropriate level of coordination.

As part of its role, Design Coordination will:

- assist and support projects as they carry out design activities
- maintain policies, guidelines and standard documents
- coordinate, prioritise and schedule design activities
- review, measure and improve design activities.

There are some areas that are out of scope for Design Coordination. The process is not responsible for:

- coordinating activities outside of Service Design
- actually carrying out Service Design activities – this is done by the various processes with guidance from Design Coordination.

 Value

This process delivers value by improving the consistency and quality of service designs and design outputs.

Many organisations have multiple project teams with internal and external staff working on designs, so the outputs can vary considerably. Having a set of guidance and a coordinating process will help to reduce the amount of rework required.

Ultimately, better service designs mean a better service, which means happier customers and users.

 Concept: Service Design Package

Part of the scope of Design Coordination is making sure the Service Design Package (SDP) is produced and handed over to Service Transition in the agreed format.

The SDP is defined as a set of *'documents defining all aspects of an IT service and its requirements through each stage of its lifecycle. An SDP is produced for each new IT service, major change or service retirement'*.

The SDP needs to include information for Service Transition, Service Operation and CSI.

Standard SDP contents will include:

- requirements
- service design, including functional requirements, Service Level Requirements and service topology
- metrics
- organisational readiness assessment
- requirements for new or changed processes
- service lifecycle plan – including definitions and requirements for transition and operation
- service acceptance criteria.

 Process activities

The following figure (*Figure 23*) shows the main Design Coordination activities for Service Design overall, and for each individual design.

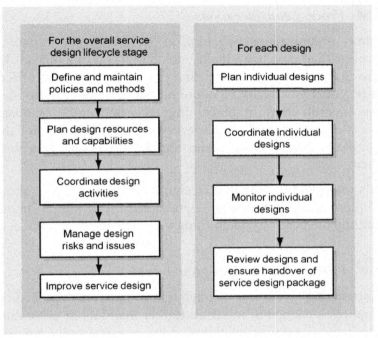

Figure 23: Design Coordination

The Design Coordination process provides vital support for design team leaders and project managers who may be technical experts in their field, but not necessarily experienced in the standards and requirements for a particular organisation.

Making sure that all projects follow standard procedures and produce standard deliverables also makes measurement across projects and value-tracking simpler.

Process considerations

Many organisations will look at the Design Coordination process and say 'we already do that!' This might well be the case; if you have an existing project management office, then you may already be coordinating designs. If there isn't any coordination in place, implementing some standard ways of working will make everyone's life easier – for the people preparing deliverables and for the people receiving them.

It's important to note that Design Coordination is not about implementing unnecessary bureaucracy. It's simply about finding the best way to do things, and getting things done.

 Putting Service Design to work

Introducing a Service Design ethos into an organisation requires a change of mindset. Rather than lots of individual projects working without any centralised control, organisations need to see all projects as being linked and producing deliverables that may ultimately need to integrate with each other.

Checklists can be your friend when introducing better design practices. If project teams and designers aren't used to considering requirements from an availability, capacity, security, etc. perspective – give them a checklist. They will be able to see what they need to consider quickly and simply.

If you're struggling to get any investment for design improvements, look at the cost of getting design wrong. Has your organisation implemented any new or changed services that failed due to design flaws? How much of the operational budget is targeted towards services that didn't work on day one?

Implement design practices and processes within context. This is true for any service management process, but is particularly relevant in Service Design. If your organisation doesn't care about security for example, you will get no backing for a hugely complex and restrictive security management process. What does the business actually need?

CHAPTER 6: SERVICE TRANSITION

 ## Service Transition theory

Once a service has been designed, it will be transitioned into the live environment. Transitions need to be carefully planned and managed, as they have the potential to negatively affect live services.

The purpose of Service Transition is to make sure that new, modified or retired services meet the business expectations documented during Service Strategy and Service Design.

 ## *Scope*

Service Transition practices should lead to an organisation developing and improving its capabilities for getting new and changed services into the live environment.

Processes need to be in place for release build, test and deployment to make sure that changes do what they are supposed to do – and don't create any unnecessary problems.

The scope of Service Transition also includes the retirement of services and movement of services between providers, for example, during an outsourcing exercise.

Requirements are mapped in Service Strategy and designed in Service Design. Service Transition then needs to transfer them to make sure they are delivered in Service Operation.

Value

Effective Service Transition helps organisations to:

- deliver successful changes
- improve communication, expectation setting and confidence in changes
- reduce costs, delays, and timing and scheduling issues
- improve control of service assets and configuration items.

 Service Transition concepts

These are some of the key concepts that it is important to understand for this phase of the service lifecycle.

 Policies for Service Transition

Putting best practice into place for Service Transition, and particularly Change Management, can be one of the most controversial areas of service management. Teams and individuals who manage services may feel that they 'own' them, and resent being told what to do. They might feel that control is unnecessary, and that they know best.

There are many ways to counteract this, and a strong set of supporting policies is one of the most effective. Policies show how management expect the organisation to work, showing staff that there is commitment to Service Transition.

These are some examples of policies that will help to embed transition practices in the organisation:

- All changes must follow Service Transition processes.

- Reusable processes and systems need to be put in place.
- Controls and disciplines associated with processes need to be put in place.
- Resources are managed proactively across transitions.
- Change Management is involved early on in the service lifecycle.

 ### *Managing communication and commitment*

Communication is often one of the weak areas within Service Transition. Many organisations have a fantastic Change Management process that is working hard to assess and approve changes. However, if the process does not also include communication about the implications, benefits and usage of a change, then it is not delivering maximum value.

All of the Service Transition processes need to play their part in delivering clear, prompt communication that explains the implications, benefits and usage of a new or changed service. Effective communication should be seen as central to Change Management, and Service Transition as a whole.

The more impact a change will have on an organisation, the more communication needs to take place. The rationale, reasons and benefits all need to be explained, as well as the implementation plan and the proposed effects.

Communication needs to be targeted at the right audience. The message needs to be clear and consistent. Remember, different parts of the organisation will need to see different levels of detail and explanation.

If total honesty around a change is not possible, this must be recognised in the communication. Security considerations, for example, may prevent full disclosure around a change.

The level of commitment in an organisation – and the possible level of resistance – also needs to be factored into communication planning.

 ### The Communication Plan

One way to manage communication around a Service Transition is to develop a Communication Plan. This will allow information to be targeted in the most effective way to the various different audiences.

Every statement that is released as part of a transition should be assessed with a number of questions, including:

- When will the information be delivered? All at once, or over a set period?
- How should the information be delivered? What tone and style will be used?
- What actions need to be taken before the communication to prepare the ground?
- How and when will groups be involved in cascading information?
- Are the communications successful in overcoming any barriers?
- Has there been any consideration of the communication needs of any other stakeholders in the project?

As well as planning communication, we need to measure whether it's working. Surveys and measures should be implemented and regular monitoring should take place. This can include feedback from the recipients of the communication. Any individual who needs more personal contact or support from the Service Transition team should be quickly identified through their feedback.

 ### *Stakeholder management*

Stakeholder management is also an essential part of Service Transition. Stakeholders could be your customers, users, support staff, and the developers and third-party suppliers that you work with. Failure to manage your stakeholders can lead to poor communication, missed deliverables and failure to gain value from a transitioned service.

New or changed services need to be fully aligned to stakeholder requirements to encourage their involvement and support. Failure to identify your stakeholders can also lead to people feeling excluded, which can mean they actively resist the change when it is delivered.

Preparing a stakeholder management strategy is a way of expressing your commitment to stakeholder management, and will make sure that communication and engagement do not drop down the priority list in the middle of a busy transition.

The stakeholder management strategy is developed during Service Design, and will be handed across as one of the items in the Service Design Package.

A typical stakeholder management strategy will include details of:

- the stakeholders
- their likely interests and influences
- the project or programme and how it will engage with stakeholders
- the information that needs to be communicated

- how feedback from stakeholders will be processed.

Once we understand who our stakeholders are, we can make sure they get the information they need to enable them to support the change.

 Service Transition process: Change Management

Every organisation has to manage change. Changes come from many sources, including customer requirements, legislative or external business changes, as well as internal improvements and fixes.

New and changed IT services need to be carefully managed to ensure they transition successfully into the production environment.

Because service providers have to deal with high volumes of change, often in complex environments, they need to have processes in place that will allow them to manage change in the most efficient way possible.

 Purpose and objectives

The purpose of Change Management is to control the lifecycle of all changes, so that beneficial changes can be made with minimal disruption to services. By successfully managing change and having efficient Change Management processes in place, we can smoothly transition new and changed services into our production environment.

The Change Management process has a number of objectives. It will:

- respond to changing business requirements while minimising disruption

- manage and implement changes to make sure that services stay aligned with business needs
- make sure that changes are recorded and managed from inception through to implementation and review.

As part of its objectives, Change Management will make sure all changes are recorded. This is a really important point. If changes are not recorded, we have no way of finding out what has happened to services. This makes it very hard to restore service if a change fails.

Changes to IT assets need to be recorded in the Configuration Management System.

Finally, Change Management will try to optimise business risk. The business may be prepared to accept a risk to get a change they need, but they need to understand it before they can sign off on the risk.

 Scope

The first part of managing change effectively is to define exactly what we mean by 'a change'. Organisations need to ask questions such as:

- What kind of changes do we need to manage?
- What kind of changes do we deal with regularly?
- What kind of changes are threats to our production environment?

What constitutes a 'change' will be different for different organisations. Service providers must arrive at their own definition, based on input from IT and the business, and their past experience.

The Change Management process has a clearly defined scope. The process covers the management of changes to all configuration items across the whole service lifecycle. In other words, anything that contributes to the delivery of a service can fall within the scope of Change Management.

This could include physical assets such as servers, virtual assets such as storage, or documents such as Service Level Agreements. The scope of Change Management also includes any changes to the five aspects of Service Design.

The key to successful Change Management is to remember that no change is risk free. All changes, regardless of their size, carry some degree of risk. The smallest, simplest changes can be the ones that cause the most damage when introduced into production environments.

Figure 24, overleaf, shows the scope of Change Management. Change Management might need to work with business Change Management and supplier Change Management processes as part of its role.

Changes will come from many sources:

- Service Strategy, and in particular Service Portfolio Management, might initiate strategic changes
- Service Design, Continual Service Improvement, Service Level Management and Service Catalogue Management might initiate service changes
- Service Operation might initiate corrective changes to fix an incident or problem.

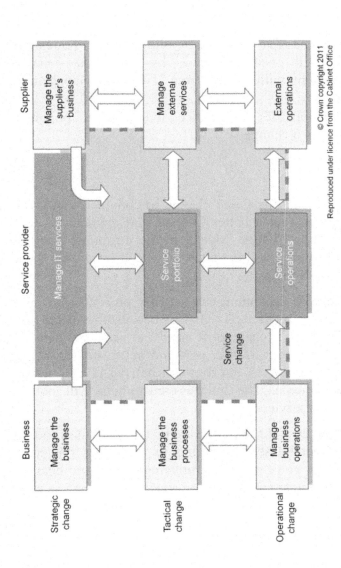

Figure 24: Scope of Change Management and Release and Deployment Management for services

There are some areas that are out of scope for Change Management. These would include:

- Business changes, such as a building move or relocation. These will be managed by business Change Management, with support from IT Change Management if necessary.
- Coordination of the service management processes involved in a change.

 Value

It may only take one failed change to convince a business of the necessity for a better Change Management process. With effective Change Management, customers can be confident that they will get what they need, when they need it and in a working state.

Poor Change Management can actually prevent a business from achieving its strategic goals – because it's frightened to ask for the IT changes it needs to support them. A business might want to offer new and improved services to its business customers, but may not believe IT can deliver the improvements. The business customers will not be offered better services.

Changes that go right first time are better for IT staff too. IT staff will spend less time trying to fix issues related to changes, and won't have to implement the same changes over and over again until they are successful.

 Concept: change proposal

A change proposal is '*a document that includes a high level description of a potential service introduction or significant*

change, along with a corresponding business case and an expected implementation schedule.'

Change proposals are normally created by Service Portfolio Management and passed to Change Management to authorise. Change Management is responsible for reviewing change proposals. They need to consider the effect on existing services, resources and any other changes happening at the same time. If the proposal is approved, it's passed back to Service Portfolio Management who will go ahead and allocate resources to the change. Change proposals usually then create individual requests for change for pieces of work. For example, a change proposal for a new service might spawn requests for change to implement new hardware, install applications, implement links to other services, etc.

 Concept: change/request for change/change record

It is important for ITIL practitioners to understand these definitions and use them appropriately. All ITIL processes must use terminology consistently to avoid confusion.

- **Change:** this is defined as the *'act of adding, modifying or removing anything that could have an effect on IT services'*.
- **Request for change (RFC):** *'a formal proposal for a change to be made'*, including all details. This will be recorded on paper, or in a service management tool. RFCs are only used to submit the request itself – further details are then added to the change record.
- **Change record:** a *'record containing the details of a change'* throughout its lifecycle. Records are created for all requests for change, even if they are rejected. The

change record contains information from the RFC and updates from Change Management as the change lifecycle progresses.

 ## Concept: types of change request

Service providers will have to deal with different levels of change. The Change Management process steps will vary depending on whether the change is classed as high impact, medium impact or low impact, and it will also vary based on the level of risk associated with a particular change.

For very high-impact and high-risk changes, senior business management approval could be required. The change may be specially managed by a cross-functional project management team. The project will then raise individual requests for changes to IT services, as necessary.

Low impact and risk changes, such as minor repairs, may be handled in a pre-defined, streamlined way, with no need for individual assessment. Change Management should, however, be involved in defining and pre-authorising these low-impact, low-risk changes.

For each organisation, the service provider will need to define the different levels of change and work out the most appropriate way to handle them. There are three main types of change: standard, normal and emergency.

Standard changes

A standard change is a change to a service or the infrastructure for which an approach has been agreed and pre-authorised by Change Management. A procedure will be defined and accepted within the organisation for this low-risk, low-impact type of change.

The authority for recording and carrying out standard changes can be delegated, for example, to the Service Desk manager. As Change Management processes mature, more and more standard changes will be identified and authorised.

There are some crucial elements of standard changes. A standard change must have a defined trigger, it must be low risk and it must be carried out using a proven, documented procedure.

Approval for standard changes is given in advance when the change is pre-authorised. Authorisation for each individual standard change can then be delegated to a nominated authority. For example, the team leader of the Service Desk might be authorised to allow the installation of a piece of standard business software. However, they will need to check that a licence is available each time a request is made.

Typical examples of standard changes include: setting up a new user, changing someone's level of access to a system, or installing a pre-approved software application.

Normal changes

Normal changes are triggered by a request from a change initiator. Normal changes may be higher risk than a standard change, or may be a change that has not been experienced previously within the organisation.

The process for handling a normal change allows the organisation to ensure the change is fully assessed by relevant stakeholders.

Assessment means that any potential difficulties are identified and addressed before the change is implemented. Typical examples of normal changes could include: the installation of an organisation-wide upgrade to an existing application, or approval for a brand new application.

Hardware upgrades, or the release of a new piece of hardware such as a mobile device, could also be classed as a normal change.

Emergency changes

Emergency changes should be much less frequent than normal and standard changes. They happen in response to major incidents or failures affecting a business critical service.

Although these changes are emergencies, they still need to be designed, managed and tested as much as possible within the time available, to ensure that they don't have a negative impact on the organisation. Even if a service is unavailable, it's still possible to make the situation worse – perhaps by spreading the impact to another service or prolonging the downtime.

Because of the urgent nature of the situations that can trigger an emergency change, some details may need to be recorded retrospectively – after the change has been implemented. This is allowable, but all the necessary details must be recorded.

Carefully defined levels of authority must be put in place within the organisation to manage emergency changes. For example, a small group of empowered people, or a senior manager, can analyse the situation quickly and provide a well-reasoned response.

Change categories

Changes may also be categorised as major, significant and minor. The categorisation will depend on the level of risk associated with the change.

 ### Concept: change model

Change models are used by organisations to document and define the specific steps required to manage a particular type of change. Models are repeatable ways of doing something. They are used by service management processes such as Change Management and Incident Management.

Once a model has been carefully defined, it should be automated using a support tool, to help remove the possibility of any human errors. Automation of the model also allows it to be measured more easily – how many times has it been used? What was the success rate?

A model will typically include:

- details of the steps to be taken
- the timescales involved in each step, and chronological order in which they need to be carried out, including dependencies
- the roles and responsibilities of the people involved

- the limitations of each role – what are they not authorised to do?
- any dependencies or actions that have to occur in a specific order
- thresholds
- how escalations should be managed, including escalation points and procedures.

As the Change Management process matures, more and more models can be defined to support the efficiency and effectiveness of managing changes. If a report highlights a particular type of change is happening frequently, it can be assessed to see if it is a good candidate for a model.

Standard changes and change models are not the same thing. Standard changes will often have a change model as part of their agreed approach, but change models can also be applied to normal and emergency changes where there are specific steps that need to be carried out.

Concept: remediation planning

Not all changes go according to plan. It is important to plan what to do if things go wrong during change implementation. This planning is known as remediation planning, in other words, what we do when a change fails.

Remediation could include invoking a back-out plan to remove the change, initiating IT Service Continuity Management, or taking other actions to protect the business process affected.

All changes must have a remediation plan. The change implementation plan will include triggers and decision points. For example, if a step isn't completed in the agreed time, the remediation plan will be invoked.

Some changes cannot be backed out. These need a different approach for remediation, and can be higher risk than changes which can be easily removed. If the change fails, a fix needs to be found that restores the service required by the business.

Concept: Change Advisory Board

The Change Advisory Board (CAB) is the group of stakeholders and knowledge holders that meet to review and support Change Management during the assessment, prioritisation and scheduling of changes.

The CAB will meet regularly, typically on a weekly basis. The actual schedule will be dictated by the volume of change within the organisation. The CAB membership may be different each time, depending on the types of changes being discussed.

The maturity of the Change Management process might also affect how often the CAB meets. An immature process might lead to more frequent CAB meetings. This is because it takes more time to assess each change, and there will not be many standard changes and change models in place yet.

The change manager will normally be the chair of the CAB, and membership may include customers, users, developers, third parties and any other required attendees.

CAB meetings can be run as regular face-to-face meetings, or virtually over audio or video conferencing systems, depending on the organisation's preference. The aim is to ensure that all the correct attendees are present, regardless of their location and time zone.

As part of their role, CAB members will:

- review and approve normal changes
- be involved in reviewing standard changes periodically
- review emergency changes after they have been implemented.

The CAB is usually an advisory board, and if a decision cannot be made at CAB, the change may be escalated to senior management for their input, advice or a decision.

A standard CAB meeting agenda could include:

- reviews of failed, unauthorised and backed out changes
- reviews of new requests for change
- a review of emergency and standard changes
- a review of the Change Management process itself to assess whether any improvements can be made.

 Concept: Emergency Change Advisory Board

Emergency changes need to be implemented quickly – normally in response to a major incident, or because of a failure affecting a business critical service.

Due to the timescales involved, it is not always practical for a full CAB to meet to approve an emergency change – since it often takes too long to convene and speak to all CAB members. Remember, during a major incident there is often no time to lose. However, emergency changes still need to be carefully managed and controlled.

In this situation, a subset of the CAB called the E-CAB, or Emergency Change Advisory Board, can be convened.

The E-CAB consists of a few, select, senior people who can be quickly convened and have the appropriate level of authority to make a quick decision. E-CAB authority may be delegated, if necessary. For example, a single manager who is on call and available outside of normal service hours may fulfil the E-CAB role on their own. So, whilst an ideal E-CAB would consist of two to three people, it could on occasion be made up of just one person.

Remember: all emergency changes still need to be designed and tested as much as possible. They must also be reviewed by the full CAB after they have been implemented.

If an organisation notices an increase in the number of emergency changes, they need to investigate the reason for this trend. It might be a sign that services are becoming less stable, or it could mean that staff are using the emergency change process to circumvent the normal process.

 Concept: process interfaces

Change Management can only be effective if it has good relationships within IT and with the business. People need to be aware that Change Management exists, and need to inform the process when changes are taking place.

Firstly, Change Management needs a strong interface with the business Change Management process. Imagine your company is moving offices. This will be managed by business Change Management, but there will be many IT changes – moving infrastructure, setting up new environments, and so on. Business and IT Change Management need to work closely together to achieve success.

Other areas that work closely with Change Management include:

- **Programme and Project Management:** Change Management needs to be involved in projects as early as possible, to identify any possible impact.
- **Organisational and Stakeholder Change Management:** to check if any changes will affect the overall organisational structure or staff.
- **Sourcing and partnering:** Change Management needs to work with internal and external vendors and partners, integrating with their Change Management processes if required.

 Service management process interfaces

Change Management also has important interfaces with the other service management processes. These include:

- **Service Asset and Configuration Management:** this process provides Change Management with information about configuration items (CIs) to support impact assessment. For example, how will a change to a server CI affect other, related CIs?
- **Problem Management:** this process will raise RFCs for permanent fixes to resolve problems, and for workarounds where necessary. Problem Management will also contribute during CAB meetings.
- **IT Service Continuity Management:** changes need to be assessed to check if they will have any impact on the continuity plans in place.
- **Information Security Management:** this process will also contribute to CAB meetings, and each change needs to be assessed for any potential security implications.

- **Capacity and Demand Management:** changes will need to be assessed for their impact on service capacity and the demand they may generate. Capacity Management will also raise changes, when necessary, to optimise infrastructure.
- **Service Portfolio Management:** this process will contribute during CAB meetings, and will raise change proposals. Change Management will use the Service Portfolio during change assessment.

 Process activities

Table 14 details the features of a normal change process flow. *Figure 25*, which follows thereafter, shows an example process flow for a normal change model.

Process step	Details
Create RFC	The change initiator creates the RFC, including the business case, or any relevant business approvals. A change proposal may already have been submitted before the RFC was created.
Record	The record is created in a tool, or using manual documents
Review	Change Management checks all information is present and accepts the change. This review checks for duplicate changes or any missing information. It also checks that the change is acceptable, i.e. it meets organisational policies and is requested by someone with the right level of authority. It's possible for a change to be rejected at this point.

Assess and evaluate	This step will include consultation with stakeholders including CAB members. The configuration items and services affected will dictate who is involved in the assessment. Change Management will often maintain matrices to allow them to easily identify the stakeholders for a particular type of change. For example, a network change would be assessed by specific technical teams.
Authorise change build and test	Approval is given to allocate resources and carry-out build and test activities.
Coordinate change build and test	Change Management monitors progress and checks the change will perform as required. They don't actually carry out the activities, but have a monitoring role. If anything unexpected happens (for example the testing results are not as expected) the change may be referred back to Change Management for advice.
Authorise deployment	This will happen if the build and test have been successful.
Coordinate deployment	Change Management will monitor the deployment, to check it goes to plan and meets the set objectives for the change.
Review and close	Changes are reviewed against their original objectives. This ensures the change process is working as it should and addresses any lessons learned. For example, if a change failed, was this due to the way it was assessed? Could failure have been avoided?

Table 14: Normal change process flow

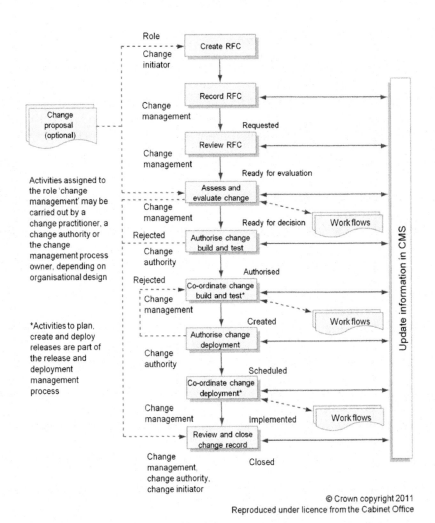

Figure 25: Example of a process flow for a normal change

Process considerations

It is very rare to find an organisation with no Change Management whatsoever. Most organisations have felt the pain of a failed change, or changes, and put some kind of process in place to try to stop it happening again. If you're looking at Change Management for your organisation, try to find out what already exists and see if you can leverage it.

It is normal to get a lot of resistance to the introduction of a more formal Change Management process. Staff might feel they have to ask permission to do their job, or feel that their skills are being doubted. It's important to sell the benefits and communicate that every change is linked and has the potential to affect service elsewhere.

You will only have one chance with Change Management. Get it wrong, and any future efforts will be met with 'we tried that and it was too bureaucratic/not effective', etc. Think carefully about the level of control that is actually needed – not too much and not too little.

The common response from technical teams during the implementation of Change Management is for them to ask 'what about x? Is x a change?' 'What about z? Is z a change?'

The short answer to this is anything that can affect services or customers is a change. You can sell the process to staff by pointing out how it will protect them, as well as protecting services; if a change goes wrong, the organisation will look at the failings in the Change Management process, not a particular team member's performance.

Service Transition process: Service Asset and Configuration Management (SACM)

IT owns, procures and manages a lot of stuff. Hardware, software, documents – it can be hard to keep track of what is deployed where, and whether it's actually being used any more. Service providers need a process to help them manage the vital kit that makes up the IT estate that supports the business.

 Purpose and objectives

The purpose of Service Asset and Configuration Management (SACM) is to control the assets used to deliver services. The process provides information on assets, such as where they are and what they are being used for. These assets are referred to as configuration items (CIs).

The process also tracks the **relationships** between assets – for example, showing how a server, database and desktop application fit together to create a service.

Service Asset and Configuration Management is about understanding all the components that make up the IT estate – whether they are hardware, software, people, documents or buildings and locations.

By understanding everything we have, and how it all fits together, we can understand our current environment, and plan the environment we want to move towards when change is required.

As part of its objectives, SACM will make sure that assets are identified, controlled and managed. This applies to all assets under IT's management. They will protect assets and services by working with Change Management to make sure that only authorised assets are used, and only authorised changes are made.

SACM manages CIs by identifying them, controlling, recording, reporting, auditing and verifying them throughout their lifecycle. They will keep accurate information about the current state of all CIs. They also need to keep historical information and planned information, to allow them to show what the infrastructure used to look like and what it may look like in the future.

The information produced by SACM is used by many service management processes. For example, Change Management needs to know which CIs will be affected by a change.

 Scope

SACM needs to manage CIs. These are the service assets that need to be managed as part of service delivery.

SACM needs to understand that all CIs are service assets, but not all service assets are CIs. For example, an application is a CI and a service asset. The experience of a particular staff member is a service asset, but cannot be managed as a CI.

SACM identifies the CIs it needs to control. The process will normally have an automated discovery tool to map CIs attached to the network, and it needs links to processes such as procurement, to find out when new CIs are coming into the organisation. Once they are identified, CIs are baselined

– which means their current state is recorded. Any changes then need to be authorised and the CI record updated.

SACM also provides a **configuration model** of services. This shows how CIs fit together to deliver a service.

The process scope may also include non-IT assets where relevant. For example, the HR records that show the training that users have received and their IT skill levels could be relevant for the delivery of services, even though they are not purely IT information.

SACM may need interfaces to other internal and external service providers. If your hardware is leased, for example, SACM could need to link to the external provider's information and change records to track what equipment is on your site.

Many organisations already have an asset register, or a process dealing with fixed asset management. SACM is more than just a list of assets, because it tracks relationships too. If an asset management process exists, SACM will need a strong interface with it and might well use its information as a starting point.

 Value

If we don't know what we've got, how can we hope to manage it? SACM tells us what we have, where it is and what state it is in. The process provides vital supporting information to other service management processes, including Availability Management, Capacity Management and Change Management.

The process will track the organisation's licence position and what software is installed where. This will prevent fines for not having enough licences, and waste caused by too many licences. This will all help to optimise services and service investment.

 ### Concept: the Configuration Management System

SACM will generate large amounts of information. For every CI, the process will store attributes such as purchase date, make, model, type, and so on. Every CI needs a unique identifier as one of its attributes.

'A Configuration Management System is a set of tools, data and information that is used to support SACM.'

SACM should be automated as far as possible, and organise its data in the Configuration Management System (CMS). Configuration records for each CI are stored in the CMS. The record will include related documents, such as Service Level Agreements, and service management records, such as related changes or incidents. The CMS is part of an organisation's overall Service Knowledge Management System.

The CMS will have different levels, including:

- **The data level:** this includes configuration records, which may be stored in repositories known as Configuration Management Database(s), or CMDB(s).
- **The integration layer:** this draws information together into an integrated configuration management database.
- **The processing layer:** this is used to query the data.
- **The presentation layer:** this is where information is given to the appropriate audience.

Different teams will use the CMS for different purposes, for example:

- the Service Desk needs information about incidents and what CIs and users are affected by them
- Change Management needs information about impact and risk related to changes to CIs
- the business may want financial information, such as the cost of CIs or their purchase date.

It's important that the CMS can supply the right information to the right audience. The supporting technology may be based around a single data-store, or links between multiple stores; it's not important as long as the CMS is fit for purpose and fit for use.

 ### Concept: Configuration Management Database

A Configuration Management System will contain one or more Configuration Management Databases (CMDBs). These databases are where configuration records are actually stored, including their attributes and relationships.

 ### Concept: configuration baseline

Once the CMS is in place, it can be used to create configuration baselines. A baseline is the reviewed and agreed normal state of a service, product or infrastructure at a given point in time.

Once a baseline is agreed, any changes need to be authorised. For example, the baseline for an organisation might be version 4.1 of an application – to progress to version 4.2 will require a request for change, assessment and authorisation.

Baselines can be used in many ways, for example, to:

- mark a development milestone for a service
- build a service to an agreed state
- change or rebuild a service: for example after an ITSC invocation
- collect the relevant components before a build
- develop a back-out plan: if the current state is not known, a change cannot be backed out.

 Concept: snapshot

The CMS also allows snapshots to be taken. A snapshot is a picture of the current state of a CI or service, and can be stored as a historical record. It is sometimes referred to as a **footprint**.

Snapshots are different to baselines because they may not be authorised and agreed. A snapshot could show unauthorised CIs that have been installed since the last baseline. These could be removed to restore the agreed, approved baseline. Snapshots can be used to:

- allow Problem Management to investigate a service issue
- allow a system to be restored
- highlight security issues, such as unlicensed or unapproved software.

 Concept: Definitive Media Library and definitive spares

Configuration management data will include references to the Definitive Media Library and the definitive spares stores. These are both physical places where hardware and software can be stored – software in the Definitive Media Library and hardware in the definitive spares.

The ITIL definitions for these terms are shown below:

Definitive Media Library (DML): *'one or more locations in which definitive and authorised versions of all software configuration items are securely stored. The DML may also contain associated CIs such as licenses and documentation. It is a single logical storage area ... '*

Definitive spares: *'an area ... set aside for the secure storage of definitive hardware spares.'*

These repositories make sure that physical configuration items and associated media are secure and controlled, so we always know where to get the items that we need.

The DML can be a complex software system hosting applications, or it can be as simple as a locked filing cabinet in each regional IT office. The level of control is what's important. It can be both physical and logical, and can be more than one instance. For example, each office may have an instance of the DML.

Figure 26 shows the Definitive Media Library and the CMS. Controlling software in this way means that we can always find the correct version to install from, and that we are not at risk from being under-licensed, or using illegitimate copies of software.

The DML also includes any documents related to the media stored there – such as licences or proof of purchase.

Clear policies need to be put in place for how hardware and software will be checked in and out of their respective stores. These policies will also address who has access to the DML and definitive spares.

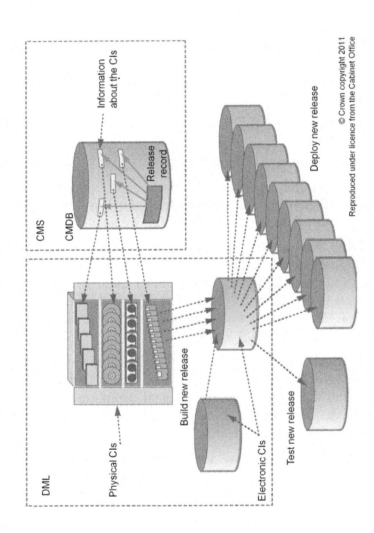

Figure 26: The relationship between the Definitive Media Library and the CMS

Software asset management

Many organisations have now introduced a policy related to software asset management (SAM). This is a process that tries to manage and protect software assets through their lifecycle, optimising the investment made at each stage. SAM tries to reduce the costs associated with owning and operating software. It also makes sure the business is not at risk of being prosecuted or fined for having unlicensed software.

There are also security benefits to be gained by making sure that only approved software is in use. The international standard related to SAM is ISO/IEC 19770-1:2012.

Effective SACM supported by a Definitive Media Library will make the introduction of SAM best practices much simpler.

 Process activities

SACM follows a five-step process:

- management and planning
- configuration identification
- configuration control
- status accounting and reporting
- verification and audit.

We're going to review the key activities in each step.

Step 1: management and planning

During this step, the important decisions are made about what needs to be done and why. The areas or services to be managed are defined, as well as the level of detail required. This will all be documented in an SACM plan, covering:

- scope
- requirements
- policies and standards
- roles and responsibilities
- systems or tools
- relationships with other processes.

There is no right or wrong way to implement SACM, and no right or wrong level of detail. It's important to understand the organisational requirements the process will meet – this will drive the way that the process is implemented.

Step 2: configuration identification

This step starts to define the types of CI that will be managed, the way they will be identified and the roles and responsibilities of the CI owners.

The attributes that will be stored for each CI need to be agreed. Every CI will have a unique identifier and type, but the other attributes will depend on the CI type. For example, hardware CIs might have 'manufacturer' as a mandatory attribute. Software might have a record of whether it has been internally developed or externally procured. The relationships between CIs will also be identified and recorded.

Discovery of CIs should be automated as far as possible, to remove the possibility of human error and reduce the overhead on resources.

Step 3: configuration control

Once CIs have been recorded, the process needs to make sure the records stay up to date. CIs will change constantly – moving location, changing owner, breaking, being updated or retired. Procedures need to be put in place to make sure changes are documented and CI records are updated.

SACM will work closely with Change Management to keep track of CIs. It can also use automated discovery tools to identify and audit changes to the IT infrastructure. For example, a nightly sweep by a discovery tool might show a new PC attached to the network. Where has it come from? SACM will initiate checks to find out.

Step 4: status accounting and reporting

Every CI has a lifecycle, tracked through changing statuses. For example, a piece of hardware may have these statuses:

- in stock
- live
- under repair
- spare
- retired.

SACM needs to put procedures in place to manage and update these status changes. This makes sure that CI records are always up to date, and organisational assets can be tracked when necessary.

The authority to update statuses can be delegated to other teams. For example, the Service Desk might update the status of a CI when it has been taken away for repair.

These updates are all done under the control of SACM, just by different resources.

This level of information has significant cost benefits for an organisation. They can track unused CIs, poorly performing CIs and identify areas for optimisation. For example, an organisation might be producing a business case for an office-wide hardware upgrade for all desktop PCs. Configuration Management can help it to identify links between the age of PCs and the frequency of their failure – this can support the financial justification.

SACM will produce reports on CIs and their status which will be used by many of the service management processes, including Change Management, Financial Management, Capacity Management, Availability Management and Incident and Problem Management.

Step 5: verification and audit

SACM needs to check that the information in the Configuration Management System reflects the live environment. These checks will take a number of different forms – from spot checks of a small portion of the infrastructure, through to full audits – perhaps held on an annual basis.

If there is a major change being planned, the organisation needs to have confidence that the CMS data being used for the impact assessment really does reflect the live environment. A major change might initiate one-off verification activity before anything is implemented.

Process considerations

SACM is theoretically an essential process for service management, because it underpins and supports so many other service management processes. How can we manage our infrastructure, if we don't know what we've got, where it is or if it's working? However, in reality, there are many service provider organisations with no SACM process – because it's too complicated, or the business case is not clear.

It's likely that there will be some Asset or Configuration Management happening in parts of your organisation already. See what exists, and whether you can use anything that's already in place.

Major projects can be a good time to implement SACM. If there is (for example) an office move or hardware refresh happening, that's a good time to start collecting data and develop a baseline. Once you have this information, it becomes a case of keeping it up to date.

The business case for SACM will always focus on indirect, rather than direct, process benefits. Think about how much more quickly incidents could be resolved, or how many more successful changes there might be. These are where you will really see the process add value.

It's very unusual to find SACM implemented in isolation. Normally, it will be implemented in conjunction with, or after, Change Management and Release and Deployment Management. Without Change Management, there is very little hope of keeping the Configuration Management System up to date.

Service Transition process: Knowledge Management

Knowledge Management focuses on supporting service delivery by making sure that the right information is always available to the right person at the right time. This helps to support successful business decision making.

In some organisations, a team will spend hours looking for a piece of information, only to find another team already has it. Alternatively, information will be needed and the organisation will realise the only person who knows has moved on, or retired. Time, money and energy is wasted when information is rediscovered over and over again.

 Purpose and objectives

The purpose of Knowledge Management is to share perspectives, ideas, experience and information. These need to be available in the right place at the right time. Organisations can be more efficient if they don't have to repeatedly rediscover the same information.

The objectives of the process are:

- to improve decision making
- to improve service quality and reduce costs by making the relevant information available when needed
- to make sure staff understand how services deliver value to customers
- to manage and maintain knowledge, information and data
- to maintain a Service Knowledge Management System (SKMS) to provide controlled access to information.

Scope

Knowledge Management is a lifecycle-wide process that helps many of the other service management processes. It has a strong relationship with Service Asset and Configuration Management, using the CMS to help inform the overall Service Knowledge Management System.

Knowledge Management is responsible for the management of knowledge and the data and information that is used to create knowledge. It is not responsible for capturing and managing configuration data – this is part of the role of SACM.

 Value

There are many benefits to the organisation when knowledge is managed properly. When knowledge is defined and procedures are in place to capture it, there is less reliance on individuals, which removes single points of failure.

Better information supports better decisions, and decisions can be made more quickly as well.

The information controlled by Knowledge Management should help staff within IT and the business to be more effective in their roles.

From a lifecycle perspective, improved knowledge transfer between lifecycle stages will lead to better services. For example, knowledge transfer from Service Transition to Service Operation will mean new services can be supported and managed from day one.

▣ *Concept: data-information-knowledge-wisdom model*

Knowledge Management is often displayed using the data-information-knowledge-wisdom model.

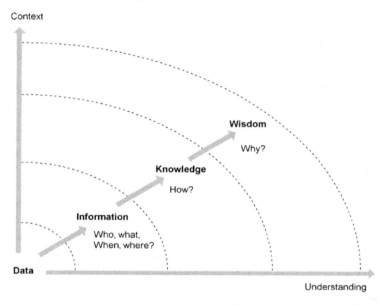

Figure 27: The flow from data to wisdom

Service provider organisations need to move away from separate data sources that are not providing value, towards a holistic perspective of their services. They should aim towards integrated information and knowledge that supports effective decision making.

Data	Data is a set of discrete facts about events.
	Most organisations capture huge amounts of data in highly structured databases, such as service management and configuration management tools, systems and databases.
	Data often tends to be unformatted. There could be a lot more data available than is actually needed to support a decision. This makes key facts much harder to identify. Knowledge Management will focus on ensuring we can capture the data we really need, as well as testing the data for accuracy.
	The correct resources need to be allocated to ensure we are capturing appropriate data. Allocating the correct resources also prevents any resource wastage on unnecessary data.
	Once we have captured appropriate data Knowledge Management will focus on transforming it into information.
Information	Information is defined as providing context to data.
	Information is typically stored in a semi-structured fashion, such as inside documents, in e-mails, and within other multi-media files – as opposed to data, which is often unformatted and raw.
	The key Knowledge Management activity around information is concerned with managing the content in such a way that makes it easy to capture, query, find, reuse and learn from experiences. This helps to ensure that mistakes are not repeated and work is not duplicated.
Knowledge	Knowledge is made up of the tacit experiences, ideas, insights, values and the judgments of individuals.

	People gain knowledge from their individual expertise and from the analysis of information and data. By combining the skills and knowledge of individuals with the available data and information, knowledge is created. Knowledge is dynamic and context based. What is considered knowledge for one service provider or function, can often be meaningless to another organisation or team. Knowledge should transform information into an ease of use form, which can facilitate decision making.
Wisdom	Wisdom makes use of knowledge to create value through educated and informed decision making. Wisdom uses context to support common sense judgement. Some of the wisdom factors that affect decision making are very hard to quantify, and wisdom may even include intangibles, such as someone's gut feeling or instincts. Wisdom can be difficult to capture and store in tools.

Table 15: Data, information, knowledge and wisdom

 Concept: the Service Knowledge Management System

Knowledge Management uses the Service Knowledge Management System (SKMS) to manage all the information it maintains.

The SKMS is underpinned by the CMS and Configuration Management Databases. It also includes additional information on areas such as user behaviour, staff skills and experience, supplier capabilities and typical user skill levels. Figure 28 shows a simplified version of the relationship between the CMDB, CMS and SKMS.

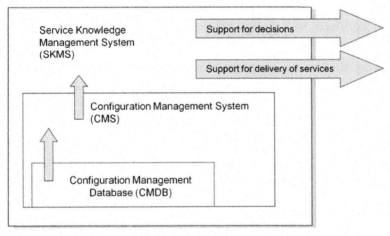

Figure 28: Relationship between the CMDB, the CMS and the SKMS

The SKMS is not one giant database and it would be a mistake to try to implement as such. It is a logical concept that joins together all service management data, information and knowledge. It will include repositories such as the Service Portfolio and Service Catalogue, Service Level Agreements and Operational Level Agreements.

Process activities

Knowledge Management needs to start with the development of a Knowledge Management strategy.

This will include a definition of what 'knowledge' is, how it will be captured, and how it will be maintained. Any legislation or regulation related to knowledge will need to be factored in, as will any organisational policies about knowledge retention and archiving.

Once the strategy is in place, Knowledge Management turns its attention to knowledge transfer. This may well involve changes to organisational culture and behaviour, encouraging staff to document and share their knowledge.

Knowledge Management also needs to put guidance in place about ongoing data, information and knowledge control and maintenance. Detailed requirements will be collected, and will drive the information architecture that is put in place. Procedures are needed to make sure that data and information is identified and collected at the right time.

Finally, Knowledge Management will raise awareness about the existence of the SKMS. If staff don't know what the SKMS is, or how to use it, the process will not deliver any benefits. Staff are more likely to develop their own local data stores, meaning less information is added to the SKMS.

 Process considerations

Knowledge Management is one of the most nebulous areas of service management. Knowledge exists in so many forms and so many places in an organisation – the idea of bringing it all under control can be a tough one to sell.

Organisations need to think creatively when it comes to Knowledge Management. How are staff sharing knowledge right now? They might be using systems or services that have previously been thought of as personal, such as social media.

It's common to find cultural barriers hampering your Knowledge Management implementation. Some staff members like to hold on to knowledge to make themselves feel valuable, safe and needed. The Knowledge Management strategy will have to address the incentives for staff to share knowledge – it could even be part of their objectives.

Too much knowledge is as bad as too little. You might have seen previous knowledge bases put in place that quickly fill up with duplicate, incorrect or irrelevant information. Proper management will prevent the organisation being overwhelmed with a wave of content.

 Service Transition process: Release and Deployment Management

Change Management is the process that controls and authorises changes. It is not responsible for the physical implementation or deployment of changes. Once a change (or group of changes) is authorised, Release and Deployment Management is the process that manages the physical build and release of the CIs that make up the change.

Purpose and objectives

The purpose of Release and Deployment Management is to plan, schedule and control the build, test and deployment of releases. They will deliver new functionality to the business while protecting existing services from any negative effects. The Release and Deployment Management process exists to ensure that the implementation of service transitions is carried out with as little possible disruption to the live environment.

A release is defined as *'one or more changes to an IT service that are built, tested and deployed together. A single release may include changes to hardware, software, documentation, processes and other components.'*

As part of its role, Release and Deployment Management will need to create and agree release and deployment plans with customers and stakeholders. They will also create and test release packages made up of CIs. A release package is *'a set of configuration items that will be built, tested and deployed together as a single release'.*

The integrity of the release package needs to be protected. Each release package will be stored in the Definitive Media Library.

Once release packages are created, they need to be deployed according to an agreed schedule. Release and Deployment Management will track and manage this process, making sure that customers and stakeholders know what is happening and when. They will record any issues or areas where the release is not performing as it should.

Knowledge transfer is an essential part of Release and Deployment Management. Customers and stakeholders won't be able to use the service if they do not receive training to aid their understanding. Operations staff won't be able to support and maintain the service if knowledge is not transferred to them.

Many releases will have a period of **early life support** scheduled. This period is normally just after the release is deployed. Extra resources are targeted to deal with any issues, and operations staff will have help from project teams and development staff. Early life support ends when Service Operation confirms they have accepted the new release.

 Scope

The scope of Release and Deployment Management includes anything needed to package, build, test and deploy a release into the live environment. This could include processes, systems and functions.

The process scope must include a formal handover to Service Operation. A release isn't complete until the operations staff have confirmed they accept it.

Any configuration item used in a release could fall within the scope of Release and Deployment Management, including:

- physical and virtual assets: such as a server or virtual server
- applications and software
- training: for users and IT staff
- services and any related contracts and agreements.

One area that is out of scope for Release and Deployment Management is carrying out testing. Release and

Deployment Management needs to make sure testing takes place, but it is physically carried out by a separate testing process. This makes sure that test results are independent and not biased.

Neither does Release and Deployment Management authorise changes. It will need authorisation from Change Management as a release progresses. Many organisations confuse Release and Deployment Management and Change Management. It is important to define the scope of each process clearly: Change Management is the process that authorises changes to the environments under their control; Release and Deployment Management decides on the best implementation approach for one or more changes.

 Value

An effective Release and Deployment Management process complements Change Management. Changes that have been authorised can be delivered quickly, within the required cost and risk parameters.

The process will make sure that all projects, programmes and implementations follow a consistent approach and keep customers informed about what is happening and when. Support staff will also get the information they need to manage the new or changed service.

 Concept: release policy

A release policy will be defined for one or more services; it will provide guidance on how and when releases are carried out.

Release policies will typically include:

- naming and numbering conventions for releases
- roles and responsibilities during a release
- release frequency
- the criteria for handover to Service Operation.

The release policy also outlines the three different types of release:

- **Major releases:** which affect large parts of the infrastructure or a service. For example, a new operating system.
- **Minor releases:** which affect smaller areas of the infrastructure or a service. For example, a software update issued to one office.
- **Emergency releases:** which are typically triggered by an emergency change. For example, an anti-virus update.

 Concept: release unit

A release unit is the portion of a service or part of the IT infrastructure normally released together. For example, an organisation may choose not to install all its applications individually onto desktop PCs. It creates an image instead which can be installed more easily. This becomes the release unit for a desktop PC. Any updates to software will be deployed via updates to the PC image.

The factors that are taken into account when defining release units include the volume and frequency of changes, the level of complexity, and the resources and time required to create the unit.

Concept: deployment options

The Service Design Package will define the approach to transition a new or changed service. Common deployment options are shown in Table 16.

Big bang versus phased	
Big bang	This deploys the release to all users in all areas at once. Big bang deployments mean the new or changed service is available to everyone quickly, but do carry a degree of risk. If something goes wrong, it goes wrong for everyone.
Phased	Phased releases deploy to segments of the user base, for example, office by office. This allows initial issues to be resolved with minimal user impact, but is not suitable if two versions of a service will not co-exist, or there is a tight deadline that the release needs to be deployed by.
Push versus pull	
Push	Push releases are 'forced' out to users with the user having no choice about whether to accept the release at that point. This is suitable for releases that need to happen by a certain date, for example, an anti-virus update.
Pull	Pull releases allow the user to choose when to accept the release. If the release has to be deployed to all users, there will be an audit after a set time to make sure everyone has pulled it down. Any user who has not pulled down the release may then receive a 'push' release.

Automated versus manual	
Automated	Automated releases are managed by a deployment tool or software. The release can be scheduled, implemented and reported on with relatively little human intervention.
Manual	Human resources are required for this type of release. It's suitable when the release is complex, or requires manual steps. Manual releases are more prone to inconsistency and human error, but they can be effectively combined with other service management activities for some releases, such as early life support or user training – as the support staff are already with the user.

Table 16: Deployment options

 Process activities

Release and Deployment Management has four phases, shown in *Figure 29*, overleaf.

Phase 1: release and deployment planning

Change Management authorisation is required for this planning phase to start. Planning completes when Change Management gives authorisation for the release to be created – based on the plans that have been produced.

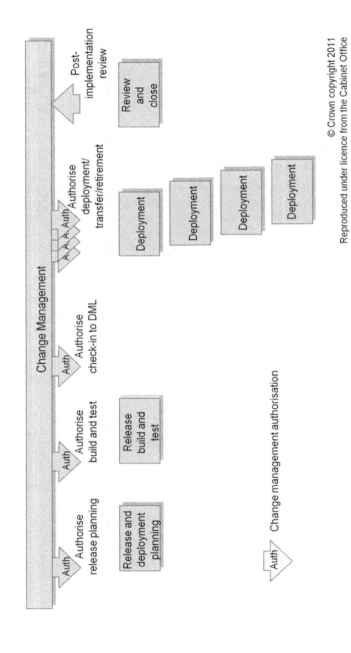

Figure 29: Phases of Release and Deployment Management

Phase 2: release build and test

This is where a release package is built, tested and placed in the Definitive Media Library.

The phase starts when Change Management authorises the build, and finishes with authorisation for Service Asset and Configuration Management to check the package into the DML.

This phase should only happen once per release.

Phase 3: deployment

Deployment is when the release package is moved from the DML into the live environment. Change Management needs to authorise the deployment, and the phase only ends when handover to Service Operation is complete.

A release might have lots of deployment phases – for example, across different sites or environments.

Phase 4: review and close

Any lessons learned or feedback about the release will be captured here, and be added to the SKMS. Any performance targets will be assessed to check whether they were met.

 Process considerations

Release and Deployment Management relies on effective Service Design. If the service design has not defined a transition approach, the process will be more likely to fail as it tries to make suitable decisions about how to deploy a new or changed service.

The process also requires close links with Change Management and Service Asset and Configuration Management. Change Management provides authorisation for deployment activities, and SACM provides information to support planning.

In many organisations, release build and test is not allocated enough time and resources in the project plan. Once development is complete, the normal way of doing things may be to rush out the release, worrying about testing, training and documentation when it's live. This is obviously not acceptable, and if this is the case, then cultural change will be required when implementing this process.

Release and Deployment Management will be more challenging in an environment with one or more third-party suppliers involved in service delivery. It is important to make sure that third-party suppliers align with any release policies implemented within the organisation, and track their compliance.

The organisational attitude to early life support can also affect Release and Deployment Management. Early life support should end when Service Operation confirms it will accept the service, because it is performing as it should. In many organisations, early life support is defined by a time period, not by quality standards. Early life support ends after (for example) two weeks, whether the service is performing well or not. This can lead to a rift between transition and operation staff. Early life support must be based around service performance, not time.

The challenges associated with Release and Deployment Management (and many other service management processes) will evolve as technology evolves. Cloud computing and software as a service (SaaS) may make the process simpler, if applications are hosted centrally. Bring your own device (BYOD) allows users more control of the hardware they access services from, and so will make the process more complicated.

 Service Transition process: Service Validation and Testing

Testing is often the part of a transition that suffers when other areas overrun. If development has taken more time or budget than expected, there is a temptation to treat the time and funds allocated to testing as 'contingency' that can be used elsewhere.

Having a formal testing process is a way of showing the organisation how important testing is and that there is a commitment to carrying out proper testing.

 Purpose and objectives

Service Validation and Testing seeks to validate and assure that any new or changed service will provide the appropriate levels of utility and warranty. By doing this, it creates confidence that the release will actually deliver the intended outcome, and will deliver within the set timescales and budgets.

The process will also provide early warning of any potential gaps between the customer requirements and the service actually being delivered. If there are going to be any differences, expectations need to be managed and the right level of communication provided. The process can be seen as quality assurance. It provides comfort that a service is fit for purpose and fit for use, and will support customer objectives.

 Scope

The scope of the Service Validation and Testing process is to support other processes such as Release and Deployment Management and Change Evaluation by quality assuring services (and service providers where necessary).

By validating that service providers have the capability, resources and capacity to deliver a service, levels of warranty and utility can be communicated with confidence.

Testing provided by the process can apply to in-house or externally developed services, including hardware, software or knowledge-based services.

Change Evaluation uses the output from testing to decide whether the service is delivering the service performance with acceptable levels of risk.

 Value

Service failures cost time and money to correct, and can damage the reputation of the service provider.

Service Validation and Testing will give the service provider and their customers confidence that the service can deliver what it's supposed to deliver. If the service will not fully meet its objectives, the process provides a full understanding of the level of risk and any shortfalls.

Remember: testing is not a 100% guarantee, but it does give improved confidence that a service can be relied upon.

 Concept: test model

A test model includes a definition of what will be tested, the test plan and the test scripts. Test models make sure that tests are carried out in a repeatable, consistent way.

As an organisation's testing capabilities improve, they will develop a library of reusable test models. This will reduce the amount of time spent developing tests, and means testing can be completed more efficiently.

 Process activities

Figure 30, overleaf, shows an example of a validation and testing process. You can see how (like most transition processes) Service Validation and Testing relies on inputs from Service Design. If any information from the Service Design Package is missing or incomplete, the testing may be applied to the wrong areas, or may miss key points.

Testing will typically address areas including:

- usability
- availability
- capacity
- security
- continuity
- compliance
- operational performance
- supporting processes
- service level performance.

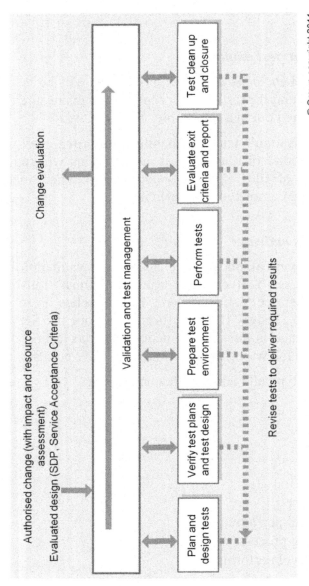

© Crown copyright 2011
Reproduced under licence from the Cabinet Office

Figure 30: Example of a validation and testing process

The levels required for each of these areas will be defined during Service Design, giving Service Validation and Testing a baseline against which to test.

The testing process will be carried out in stages, defined by sets of exit and entry criteria. The exit criteria from stage one will be the entry criteria for stage two. For example, confirmation that the test environment is ready will trigger testing activities.

Process considerations

The independence of testing is crucial. It's good practice to use separate resources for development and testing of a new or changed service where practical. Developers know what a service is meant to do, so may be able to work around unexpected results in ways a user could not. They might also be tempted to ignore failures in favour of meeting a deadline.

The test environment is an area that requires careful consideration. It needs to reflect the live environment, so it will need to be updated when changes are approved and implemented. This needs to be considered when the scope of Change Management is being agreed.

Data in the test environment needs to be protected in the same way that live data is, and licensing also needs to be addressed – some software provides licences for test environments free of charge, but others do not.

From an operations perspective, the test environment can look like an extension of the spares storage area. When a piece of the live infrastructure breaks, it's tempting to grab something from the test environment that isn't currently in use. This is a dangerous path to go down. The test environment must be protected, so that the testing carried out delivers valid results.

 Service Transition process: Change Evaluation

Changes don't always do what they are supposed to do. A change introduced to fix a problem might only address it partially, or might cause problems elsewhere. Organisations need an objective process to assess the intended and the unintended effects of the changes they implement. This process is Change Evaluation.

 Purpose and objectives

Change Evaluation provides a formal approach to determine how a service change will perform. This includes assessing its impact on business processes, and on other IT services. The actual change performance can then be compared to its predicted performance, and risks and issues can be identified and managed.

An effective Change Evaluation process will help to set stakeholder expectations about what the change will actually do – it may not be the magic bullet that will fix everything.

The process will try to assess any unintended change effects, and it will provide reports to Change Management during the lifecycle of a change, that support decisions about authorisation.

 Scope

During the lifecycle of a change to an IT service, there will be a number of authorisation points or gateways.

For example, authorisation may be granted to proceed to deployment if testing has gone well – or withdrawn if testing has not performed as expected.

Change Evaluation provides a formal approach to support change authorisation. It will normally be applied to larger, high risk and impact changes. Lower risk and impact changes will be assessed via the normal Change Management process. Change models for each type of change should define whether to involve Change Evaluation.

 Value

If you've seen time and resources wasted on a change that did not deliver business value, you will understand why Change Evaluation is important.

If we can assess our current changes in terms of the impact to the business, we will gain valuable information to be able to assess changes more effectively in the future. Resources can be targeted towards implementing the changes that will deliver maximum business value.

 Concept: evaluation report

During the lifecycle of a change, interim evaluation reports are produced – for example, after evaluation of the predicted performance is complete.

If the change will not meet its objectives, the interim evaluation report may prompt Change Management to reject the change. If the change will meet its objectives, the interim evaluation reports will be built into the final evaluation report produced when the change is completed.

A typical report will contain:

- **Risk profile:** including residual risk after change implementation.
- **Deviations:** the difference between actual and predicted performance.
- **Qualification statement:** if needed.
- **Validation statement:** if needed.
- **Recommendation:** about whether the change should be accepted or rejected.

 Process activities

Figure 31, overleaf, shows the process flow for Change Evaluation.

The inputs are very important – for example, if Change Evaluation has not received the Service Design Package, it will be very hard to assess what the change is actually meant to do.

The interfaces between Change Evaluation and Change Management need to be clearly defined.

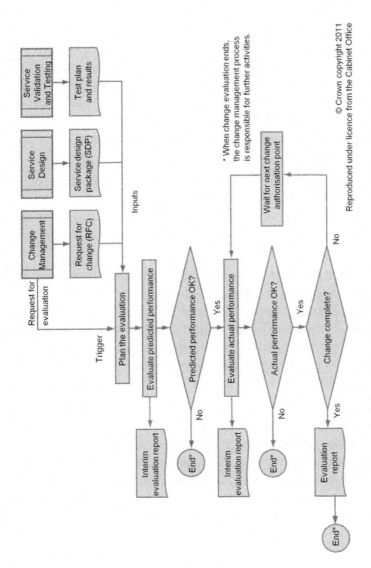

Figure 31: Change Evaluation process flow

© Crown copyright 2011
Reproduced under licence from the Cabinet Office

Process considerations

Organisations need to carefully consider and document which changes the Change Evaluation process will be applied to. For small, low-impact and low-risk changes, a full evaluation will be a waste of resources. For larger, high-impact and high-risk changes, the process can be essential to prove that the change delivered the intended outcomes and has provided a return on investment.

Change Evaluation can only go on for a limited period of time. The unintended effects of a change may materialise months after it has been implemented, but it's not practical to keep the process working indefinitely. A cut-off point should be agreed, so that the maximum information is captured within a realistic timescale.

Many organisations will not understand the purpose of the Change Evaluation process, if they are already doing Change Management. The process objectives and scope will need to be defined, communicated and agreed. The focus is on the business value the change should deliver. This is where Change Evaluation adds its own value to the management and assessment of future changes, by highlighting areas for process and design improvement.

In some organisations, Change Evaluation is implemented as a subset of the Change Management process activities, rather than being viewed as a separate process. This may be appropriate in smaller organisations, or if there is a feeling of 'process overload' in the organisation that might lead to resistance during implementation.

Service Transition process: Transition Planning and Support

During Service Design, the Design Coordination process provides structure and consistency across teams and projects. In Service Transition, Transition Planning and Support works in the same way. Individual transitions need to be viewed centrally, so that resources can be managed and prioritised.

 Purpose and objectives

The Transition Planning and Support process coordinates the overall planning for transitions and any resources that are involved. It has a number of objectives. It will plan and coordinate resources, and coordinate activities across teams. It will also make sure that any cost, quality or time estimates are met.

Transition Planning and Support creates a framework of reusable practices and documents that can save lots of time during a transition. It will make sure that plans are produced and available to customers and stakeholders as required, as well as providing risk management across processes and transitions.

Transition Planning and Support will also monitor and improve the performance of Service Transition processes as a whole.

 Scope

The scope of Transition Planning and Support includes guiding changes through the Service Transition processes, and coordinating resources and workloads. This is particularly relevant when there are many changes happening at once, and priorities need to be managed.

The process will work with programme and project management teams, Service Design and development teams to make sure that the value designed into services is transitioned into operations.

It will plan for the budget and resources required, and try to improve Service Transition performance on an ongoing basis.

Remember: Transition Planning and Support does not physically carry out Service Transition activities – it just coordinates them. For example, they do not build a release, but they will coordinate the processes involved and any associated resources required.

Value

The Transition Planning and Support process introduces consistency during transitions – whether they involve internal or external resources, new or changed services. This allows service providers to manage high volumes of changes and releases with confidence.

Standardised transition planning makes it easier to compare 'apples with apples' and assess how different transitions perform in relation to each other.

Process activities

The overall organisational transition strategy will govern Transition Planning and Support (TPS) activities. The strategy outlines the organisational approach for transitions, including purpose, objectives, context, stakeholders, scope, requirements and deliverables.

TPS will prepare for individual transitions by checking the inputs from other lifecycle stages, and raising and scheduling RFCs. They will plan and coordinate Service Transitions, within the context of other transition activity happening in the organisation.

During a transition, the process provides ongoing support to project teams and stakeholders, including administration related to changes, risks and carrying out reporting, etc.

 Process considerations

Any organisation that thinks Transition Planning and Support is just an 'admin function' is missing the point. The standardisation that the process brings will help all transitions to progress more smoothly, using consistent working practices and procedures.

TPS needs to work with internal and external stakeholders, particularly when there are third parties involved in delivering all, or part of, the transition. If the process is seen as purely administrative, it will be more difficult to establish and maintain these relationships at the right level.

Most organisations will have more than one transition happening at once. TPS provides a central point of coordination for all transitions. When there is conflict between resources, the process makes it much easier to prioritise what should be allocated where.

Putting Service Transition to work

Service Transition can be the squeezed middle part of the service lifecycle in many organisations. Poor quality outputs are handed over from Service Design, and the business demands the new service goes into operation as soon as possible. The more pressure on Service Transition, the more important proper processes become.

Most organisations are doing some kind of Change Management – it only takes one or two major change failures for the process to be implemented. Improving your current Change Management process can be a good starting point for other processes, such as Service Asset and Configuration Management, and Release and Deployment Management.

Getting the size and scope of your transition processes right is critical. The transition processes often meet resistance as they are seen as slowing change down and introducing bureaucracy. Applying just the right amount of control to each type of transition will help to prevent this resistance.

One area that many organisations struggle with is how and when to get processes, such as Change Management, involved with their projects. The short answer is – as early as possible. The change manager doesn't need to sit in on every project meeting, but they do need to know what projects are happening, and be kept appraised of key information, e.g. objectives and timescales.

Finally, be aware and communicate very strongly that Service Transition processes are not magic bullets that will instantly fix everything. As you start to put good practice into place, you might even see more failed changes recorded. This could just be because you're actually finding out about them, rather than before when they would be implemented, fixed and hushed up. Keep your stakeholders informed about the progress you're making, and highlight any issues that have been caused by areas outside your control – for example poor quality inputs from design and development teams.

CHAPTER 7: SERVICE OPERATION

 Service Operation theory

Services only deliver value once they are live and being used by customers to achieve business outcomes. The purpose of Service Operation is to undertake activities and processes to manage and deliver services at the levels agreed with business users and customers.

Service Operation manages the technology used to deliver services and collects information on service performance, and other defined service metrics. Service Operation is vital for effective service management. Services can be well designed and transitioned smoothly, but they still need to be managed in the live environment to ensure they keep working well.

 Scope

Service Operation covers all areas of service delivery, including:

- services
- service management processes
- technology
- people.

 Value

Effective Service Operation processes and functions help organisations to:

- reduce the impact and frequency of outages
- provide access to standard services
- provide data to justify investment.

 Service Operation concepts

 Balance in Service Operation

Balance is vital for Service Operation. This lifecycle stage is expected to deliver stable services, often during periods of great change. There are four main areas where Service Operation needs to achieve balance.

Stability versus responsiveness
The first area where balance needs to be achieved is stability versus responsiveness.
Customers expect the operational environment to be stable and well supported, but at the same time, the business expects improvements and minor changes to be implemented quickly.
Service Operation needs to provide a protected environment that meets service targets, whilst still implementing the improvements that support the business.
Internal IT view versus external business view
By its very nature, Service Operation needs to have a close understanding of the technology used to provide services, so it can manage and control it. However, reports and outputs to the customer must be from the service perspective, as the customer may not understand the information if it is given at component level. Components of the infrastructure need to be mapped to the services they provide to allow accurate reporting.
Service Operation departments that focus too much on technology may become unresponsive to customer needs and

will have a very siloed viewpoint. They may be organised into teams based on the different types of technology available. Organisations that are inward looking in this way find it very difficult to translate the customer- and service-based requirements into technical terms, as they focus on individual components, not the end-to-end view.

Organisations that focus too much on the external business view may end up promising something that the technology is unable to deliver – for example, wireless networks are desirable to many customers, but are restricted for security reasons in some organisations.

Service Operation staff need to understand what is possible, before they offer customers opportunities to access different types of technology.

Reactive versus proactive

Reactive support is about fire-fighting. It is defined by lack of planning, instability and periods of downtime. Improvements are not identified and resource utilisation is dictated by what incidents are occurring on the infrastructure.

Proactive support entails planning ahead, and involves identifying improvements before the business is affected. Proactive operational management is characterised by planning and use of techniques, such as component failure impact analysis and fault tree analysis.

All organisations need a balance of reactive and proactive operational management and support. Things go wrong, and we need to be prepared to deal with incidents quickly and effectively. However, we should also be proactive and plan ahead – hopefully reducing the amount of time we have to spend doing reactive support. If an organisation finds it has gone too far out of balance here, the culture and management system should be assessed – for example, are we rewarding reactive behaviour, or are we not allocating resources for proactive activities?

Service quality versus service cost
Service providers can provide 100% availability for any service, but only if they are prepared to spend the money associated with this level of service.
Service Operation needs to understand the service targets set as part of Service Strategy and Design, then manage and meet these in a cost-effective way. Levels of service and operational costs need to be reviewed regularly to ensure they meet customer requirements.
Cost and quality can also be influenced by the business or customer budget. Some service providers offer a bronze, silver and gold set of services depending on the customer's budget and needs.
Customers want to feel that they are paying a fair price. This may be based on industry comparisons, the price last year or just individual perception. Service providers need to balance cost and quality to meet customer expectations – or be able to provide cost information if the customer has unrealistic expectations.

Table 17: Balance in Service Operation

 Communication

Communication is a key concept for Service Operation because their activities are often carried out by many different functions, meaning cross-functional communication is required.

Communication is also relevant within Service Operation because this is the stage of the lifecycle where we have the most contact with our customer – potentially thousands of contacts a day through channels such as the Service Desk.

In their quest to continually improve and offer better and better support to their customers, many organisations are looking at new ways to communicate.

Allowing customers to log their own incidents isn't new, but this area has recently expanded to include access to support systems from mobile devices.

For example, imagine if a user was able to take a photo of their application error using their phone, and then upload the image to the Service Desk via social media.

Service providers must evaluate how they communicate with their customers and see if the methods they are using are still fit for purpose.

Example: Evaluating communication methods

Service Operation is often made up of a number of different functions and roles. Service Operation also often covers long service hours, providing out-of-hours support and managing back-ups, batch jobs and overnight print runs. Because of this, Service Operation has to ensure that communication between functional areas and different shifts is well managed. This communication can take the form of handover reports, logs, timesheets and workflows, incident updates and reports. When a team is split over different offices or countries, this is even more important, as staff may never get the chance to talk face-to-face

The main points to emphasise about communication are that the interfaces must be defined, communication channels, types and frequencies must be agreed, and the efficiency of communication needs to be regularly reviewed.

Examples of Service Operation communications that need to be managed include:

- routine operational communication
- communication on shift handover or shift change
- performance reporting
- communication in and between project teams and resources
- communication related to changes
- communication related to exceptions or deviations from the norm
- communication related to emergencies
- training on new or customised processes and service designs
- communication of strategy and design to Service Operation teams.

Good communication can actually prevent or mitigate issues. Organisations should develop an overall communication policy to provide guidance and direction.

 Providing good service

A good service provider provides good service. It sounds obvious, but it's not that easy. Organisations that provide good service will be results focused and target driven, and they will constantly review how they interact with their customers, to identify opportunities for improvement.

By considering how we are providing service, we focus on a number of different behaviours. We need to ensure we are timely, professional and courteous in our dealings with our customers.

Strong customer relationships need to be built at all levels of the organisation, from senior management down to operational staff. If we don't have strong relationships with customers, they will be reluctant to provide information that will help us fix and improve IT services.

For example, imagine if you have a staff member at the Service Desk who is discourteous when dealing with customers. Each customer this staff member deals with will be left feeling upset or annoyed. The customer will leave with a much lower perception of the IT department.

If a second-line support person needs to visit the customer (for example, to fix their PC), they will find the customer is already hostile when they get there. They will have a difficult customer interaction, which could well lead to a poor customer satisfaction rating. Bad attitudes have a way of spreading.

It's important we remember that we are not just providing an IT service; we are providing a customer service as well.

 ### Concept: operational health

Service Operation plays a key role in measuring the operational health of an organisation and the services it provides.

The majority of organisations now depend heavily on their IT service and infrastructure. This massive dependence on IT has made the IT infrastructure a critical 'organism' needed for the business's survival. Treating the infrastructure as an organism means that vital signs can be isolated within it. These vital signs are defined as critical to the successful execution of the organisation's critical functions. They could include items such as network bandwidth utilisation, storage capacity and CPU utilisation. If these vital signs are operating within expected, or normal, ranges, then IT is healthy and does not require additional attention.

Vital signs for measuring the operational health of a service should be established in Service Design, then tested and refined in Service Transition, monitored with Service Operation and optimised by Continual Service Improvement as needed. Service Operation monitors the vital signs for each live service.

Operational health is dependent on the ability to prevent incidents and problems. Proactive health management of services, a component of Problem Management, should be employed to perform diagnostic checks to identify potential issues that would affect these vital signs later on.

These types of checks may involve activities such as the timed replacement of infrastructure near the end of its guaranteed life, to help ensure that reliable and maintainable infrastructure is sustained.

When unexpected faults do occur, operational health depends on the ability to use Incident and Problem Management to identify the source of faults quickly, so that they have minimal impact on the service.

 Involving operations staff in design and transition

In smaller organisations, the staff that carry out Service Operation activities may be the same people as the staff doing design and transition work. In larger organisations, staff are placed into more specialist roles. In this type of structure Service Operation staff might never get any involvement with design activities. If this is the case, line managers should plan to expose their staff to other lifecycle stages.

There are two main benefits for an organisation when it involves operational staff in design and transition activities:

- Operational staff can help design and transition staff to avoid costly mistakes, through their greater knowledge of the live environment and end users.
- The knowledge transfer process will begin early on, ensuring that operational staff understand and are ready to support new or changed services.

Operational staff should be given objectives associated with their involvement in Service Design, and measured against them. Line managers must make time and resources available for this to happen.

 Service Operation process: Event Management

'An event is any change of state that has significance for the management of a configuration item or a service.'

Events are happening all over our infrastructure, every minute of every day. Some events need to trigger an action, others do not. The Event Management process helps to make sense of the massive amounts of data it is possible to capture using modern monitoring tools, and make sense of what we are seeing.

 Purpose and objectives

The purpose of Event Management is to be able to detect, analyse and take appropriate action in relation to events – as well as to communicate event information as required.

Successful Event Management means action can be taken to resolve events before service levels are affected. Event Management allows events to be identified before they cause incidents, allowing Service Operation staff to take proactive action.

Events are communicated by alerts. An alert is *'a notification that a threshold has been reached, something has changed or a failure has occurred'*. Alerts can be targeted towards the people who need to take action, such as specialist technical staff. They could be communicated, for example, via a dashboard, or an SMS text message.

Events can trigger off many operational processes and activities, and they need to be managed and prioritised. Event Management forms the basis of operational monitoring and control. The process will:

- detect changes of state
- determine the appropriate control action
- provide the trigger for many service management processes
- provide information to compare service performance against Service Level Agreements
- provide a basis for service reporting and improvement.

Examples of events could include:

- a monitoring tool detecting a user has logged in
- a read receipt confirming an e-mail has arrived
- a back-up is confirmed as complete
- a print job fails.

Some of these events require action to be taken. Others will not.

Scope

Event Management applies to any aspect of service management that needs to be controlled and can be automated. This could include:

- configuration items
- environmental conditions – such as air conditioning
- software licence monitoring
- security
- normal activity.

 Value

Event Management, when implemented properly, will support proactive service management. It can, for example, detect an incident before end users do, allowing it to be resolved before business processes are affected.

Event Management should also increase the level of automation used for service monitoring, meaning fewer manual resources are used to track service performance. This will save the organisation time and money.

When integrated with other service management processes, such as Incident and Problem Management, Event Management delivers even more benefits, as warnings are delivered to the right team or person at the right time. All of this should ultimately lead to better service performance and happier customers.

 Concept: monitoring versus Event Management

Event Management and monitoring are very closely related, but slightly different in nature. Event Management is focused on generating and detecting meaningful notifications about the status of the IT infrastructure and services. While it is true that event monitoring is also required to detect and track these notifications, in practice event monitoring is much broader than Event Management. For example, event monitoring tools will check the status of a device to ensure that it is operating within acceptable limits, even if that device is not generating events.

Put simply, Event Management works with occurrences that are specifically generated to be monitored. Event monitoring tracks these occurrences, but will also actively seek out conditions that do not generate events.

 Concept: types of events

Events are divided into three categories.

Informational	Informational events require no action, but are stored for future reference. Examples of informational events would include a back-up completing successfully, or a user logging into an application.
	Organisations should put a policy in place for each type of informational event to dictate where they are stored and how long they need to be stored for. They will not usually need to be kept forever.
Warning	Warning events signify unusual, but not exceptional operation. Examples of this type of event could be a print job taking longer than normal to complete, or disk space reaching a pre-defined percentage.
	Warning events need to be assessed to see if action is required. Sometimes they can be

	safely ignored, but on other occasions they show a trend of gradually worsening performance that might affect services in the future.
Exception	Exception events can often mean an SLA or OLA has been breached, and a service is not working as it should. Examples here could include a back-up job failing, or a network link not responding. Exception events will require action, and many are escalated immediately to Incident, Problem or Change Management.

Table 18: Types of events

 Process activities

Figure 32, overleaf, shows the process flow for Event Management.

Event Management relies on monitoring tools to be effective. Without good tools to support it, the process would be very manual, and the cost of the process activities would outweigh the value delivered.

The correlation and filtering of events is the stage of the process where an event's significance is decided. This will be an ongoing process, with improvements being made all the time.

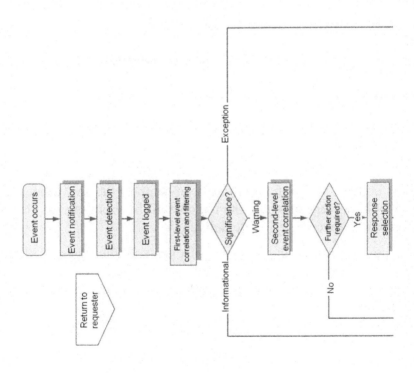

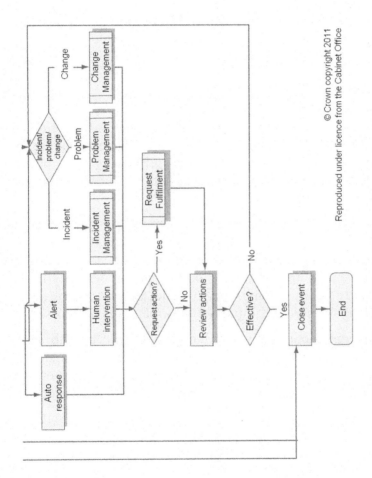

Figure 32: The Event Management process

If events are not filtered correctly, there are two main dangers. Firstly, there is a danger that an important event will be missed and service will be affected. Secondly, there is a danger that many low-level events will be forwarded on to Change, Incident and Problem Management – swamping the processes and hiding what's really important.

 Process considerations

Event Management implementations can go wrong in two main ways. The first way is when not enough information is collected. Even though the process is in place, tools aren't picking up the right events and service is still being affected. This makes it very hard to justify further investment in the process.

The second way that Event Management can go wrong is when too much information is collected and passed to operations teams; they end up swamped, and start to ignore events – even the important ones. The process needs to constantly refine what is being collected and where it is sent, to make sure the important information is not missed.

When implementing Event Management, it's best to start with a simple set of measures, and then add to them as the process matures. Incidents and problems can be used as learning opportunities to identify whether further monitoring would be beneficial.

It's also very important to publicise the success of Event Management. Because the process works proactively and can prevent incidents before they occur, there is a danger that its successes are never seen outside Service Operation. If Event Management is proactively preventing incidents and improving the level of service on offer, this should be used to justify further investment.

 Service Operation process: Request Fulfilment

A service request is a generic description for all the services needed by users that aren't actual incidents or failures. A service request is defined as *'a formal request from a user for something to be provided'*.

Service requests are often very small (or standard) changes – they are low risk and very common. Examples of service requests include:

- password changes
- access to printers
- desk changes or moves.

The Request Fulfilment process allows each service request to be effectively managed without causing unnecessary strain or bottlenecks in the Incident and Change Management processes.

 Purpose and objectives

The purpose of Request Fulfilment is to manage the lifecycle of each service request. This means from the moment the request is raised through to completion and fulfilment. Request Fulfilment also needs to manage any third-party suppliers, or procurement resources, involved in fulfilling the request.

The objectives of Request Fulfilment are to:

- maintain customer and user satisfaction through efficient and professional handling of service requests

- provide a channel for users to request and receive standard services
- provide information to users and customers on the services available, and how to order them
- source and deliver services
- assist with general information, complaints and comments.

 Scope

In most organisations, requests are received by the Service Desk staff. Many teams can be involved in fulfilling a service request, including procurement teams, facilities and even teams within the business areas, such as finance and human resources.

The Service Desk team will decide if a contact is an incident or a service request and follow the Incident Management or Request Fulfilment process, handling each incident or request in the best possible way.

Some organisations don't differentiate between incidents and service requests at all. This can cause problems because the SLA targets are usually different, and it can also make reports and management information less meaningful.

For example, a request to provision a laptop will usually have a much longer SLA target than a request to fix a laptop. A report showing lots of contacts related to laptops will be hard to decipher – is the organisation seeing a lot of broken laptops, or is it seeing lots of requests for them?

Value

Request Fulfilment allows users to understand what is available to them, how to request standard services and how quickly they will receive them. This reduces the number of requests for non-standard items, and can help to prevent users going out and buying their own devices.

Centralising the management of service requests should allow some consolidation of suppliers and contracts as well, which can lead to cost savings for the organisation.

 Concept: request model

Most organisations will see the same types of service request over and over again. Models are developed to provide a repeatable and consistent way of dealing with requests, such as new-user account creation, provision of a laptop or provision of a projector. The model will document steps to be taken, timescales, roles and responsibilities, and the necessary permissions.

As the Request Fulfilment process matures, more and more models will develop.

 Concept: self-service

Where possible, the Request Fulfilment process should be automated to allow users to request services via a web front-end. This will typically present users with a standard set of options, and makes sure the right data is captured. If line manager authorisation is required, this can also be collected automatically.

Self-service technology for service requests will reduce the number of errors during request recording. It will also mean that fewer resources are required to manage the process, and will provide excellent information for analysis.

Process activities

Figure 33 shows the typical Request Fulfilment process flow. Requests may be for information or advice, about access to a service, or for a standard change.

Requests will be logged using a tool or manual process. The information captured needs to include, at a minimum:

- identifying number (unique identifier)
- category
- urgency and impact
- priority
- name of requestor
- approvals (where appropriate)
- details of request
- cost centre (where appropriate)
- status
- date and time stamps.

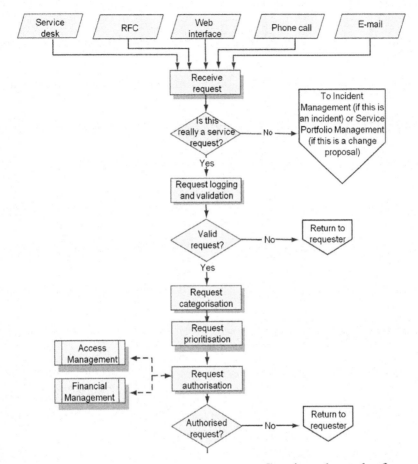

Continued overleaf ...

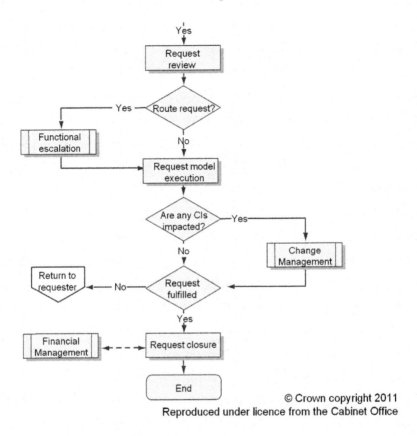

Figure 33: Request Fulfilment process flow

 Process considerations

As with many service management processes, when you implement Request Fulfilment, keep it simple. Most end users have some experience of internet shopping which will help them to understand the concept of ordering things via a webpage. However, if your users have fairly basic IT literacy you need to keep things as simple as possible.

The request models you define will be very helpful when you create your workflows and user interface for Request Fulfilment. For example, you might be able to create one simple request template for 'new user', rather than expecting your requestor to know exactly what type of chair, desk, mouse, mouse mat, keyboard, base unit, monitor, etc. to ask for.

When it comes to Request Fulfilment, you need management support and you need your managers to walk the walk. It's no use trying to force everyone down a central process, if your management team are walking round with the latest shiny toys they paid for out of their own budget. If the organisational decision is that Request Fulfilment offers two types of laptop as standard, that's what your management team need to be using.

The Request Fulfilment workflows will also need to get the right level of approval in the right place. If a line manager needs to sign off a mobile device for a user, this authorisation has to be granted before procurement can start. If you don't manage authorisation carefully, you might find you've spent quite a lot of money and aren't able to recoup it from the business.

Service Operation process: Access Management

Access is the way in which customers and users are able to use services and get the functionality they need. In many organisations, this process is not well managed from start to finish.

Getting users set up is usually well managed, because they need access to services to carry out their role. Removing access when a user leaves, or changes department, might not be tracked as closely.

Effective Access Management will draw on information from many sources, including human resources. The process will be shaped by the market the organisation operates in and its attitude to security and risk. For example, a financial organisation might take Access Management very seriously.

 Purpose and objectives

The purpose of Access Management is to provide the rights for users to access services, executing policies as defined by Information Security Management.

It is important to remember that Access Management isn't setting the policy – this is done by Information Security Management during the Service Design phase. Access Management is simply carrying out and operationally managing the processes set during Service Design. The process helps to enforce security in all areas related to access.

The objectives of Access Management include:

- managing access to services based on policies and actions defined by Information Security Management
- efficiently responding to requests for access
- changing or restricting access as required
- monitoring access to make sure it is not being abused.

Scope

Access Management grants access to services in line with organisational policies. The process is normally carried out by operational teams looking after infrastructure and applications. In most organisations, there isn't a separate team of Access Management staff.

Access Management protects organisational data and intellectual property, including confidentiality, integrity and availability. The process is not responsible for making sure that services are available once access has been granted – that would fall within the scope of Availability Management.

 Value

Access Management helps to keep an organisation's information assets safe and secure. It also helps to ensure that users are productive, because they have access to what they need to do their job.

Access Management can support audits to show how services are being used (or abused), which in turn can support compliance with regulatory requirements.

 Concept: Access Management terminology

The basic concepts that support Access Management activities and policies are access, identity, rights, service groups and directory services.

Access	'Access means the level of data or functionality a user is entitled to use'. This is often dictated by the role they have within the organisation.
	If a user moves to a new team, the access they need will usually change.
Identity	Identity refers to 'the information that identifies a user', for example a user ID and password.
	A user's identity will need to be unique to them. For example, if an organisation has two users named John Smith, they might have user names jsmith and jsmith1.
Directory services	Directory services are 'a specific type of tool used to manage access'. They make the process of granting access and managing users much simpler, and will usually have reporting functionality to show who has access to what.
Rights	Rights are 'the actual settings used to provide access within a service or application – such as read, write or delete.'
Service groups	Service groups are set up for users with similar access requirements. A new starter can be added to a group to get quick access to all the services they need.

Table 19: Access Management terminology

 Process activities

Figure 34 shows the Access Management process flow.

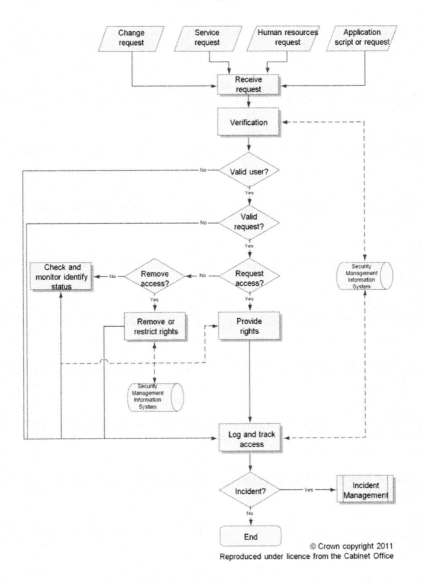

© Crown copyright 2011
Reproduced under licence from the Cabinet Office

Figure 34: Access Management process flow

It is important to remember that Access Management is simply following the policies established during Service Design – it is an administrative function, carrying out organisational directions and policies and making sure security requirements are implemented.

 Process considerations

If Access Management hasn't been considered as a single process in your organisation, you may be starting out with a bit of a mess. It's common to find a complete lack of standardisation – so one user (let's say John Smith) might exist as JSmith, Jsmith1, Johnsmith, etc. in different systems.

The first step is to try to bring order to the chaos. It's probably not going to be feasible to go back and retrospectively correct everything, but you can implement policies that will start to improve the situation in future.

The main business case for Access Management relates to security, which is high on the agenda for many organisations. If you can find examples of users who have access to things they shouldn't have, or users who have left, but still have access to systems and services, this can help you to raise the profile of the process.

Here are two examples of Access Management gone badly wrong:

An organisation had to fire an employee for breach of contract. The employee was asked to leave site immediately, but their access to services was not disabled straight away.

The employee returned home and used the 'all employees' e-mail address (also not disabled) to send an e-mail to the whole company advising them that 'dark forces' had taken over the management team.

After this, the 'all employees' e-mail address was disabled, and new processes put in place to revoke access when employees were dismissed.

Example: E-mail gone wrong

A support team member was set up with access to e-mail including some shared folders. It was six months before they realised the level of access they had been given allowed them to open anyone in the organisation's inbox and send e-mails as if from them.

Luckily, the team member reported this as soon as they realised what was happening.

The access was revoked, and an audit carried out to make sure nothing similar happened again.

Example: E-mail gone wrong again!

If you can find similar examples for your organisation, you have a good business case for better Access Management. It is fine having an information security policy, but without someone to administrate day-to-day access requests and implement the policy at the operational level, the policy will have little impact.

Service Operation process: Incident Management

An incident is defined as *'an unplanned interruption to an IT service – or a reduction in the quality of an IT service. The failure of a configuration item that has not yet had any effect on a service is also an incident.'*

An example of a CI failing without service being affected could be an instance where one of a pair of mirrored network links has failed. There is no effect on service yet – but the likelihood of a service failure has become greater because the required redundancy has been removed.

 Purpose and objectives

The purpose of Incident Management is to restore normal service as quickly as possible – minimising the downtime and impact on the business.

The process objectives include:

- making sure that standard methods and procedures are used to optimise the handling of incidents
- improving communication about incidents to IT and business staff
- improving the reputation of IT by managing incidents professionally
- prioritising incidents according to business priorities
- maintaining user satisfaction with IT service quality.

 Scope

Incidents can be reported by users, technical staff or third parties. They may also be detected by automated monitoring tools or by other processes such as Event Management, and then passed to Incident Management for resolution.

Every organisation deals with incidents every day. Systems crashing, printers not working, network devices failing, applications showing error screens – these are all typical examples of incidents. Incident Management exists to make sure that incidents are resolved as quickly as possible, ensuring end users can be productive and have access to the IT services that they need.

 Value

Good quality Incident Management delivers real benefits for the business and end users of IT services. Customers and users know that when they report an incident it will be properly recorded and dealt with in accordance with the impact to the business.

Incident records provide valuable management information, showing where services are failing and where improvements can potentially be made.

IT staff also benefit from Incident Management. Incidents are dealt with by staff with appropriate skills (such as first-, second- or third-line support) and there is no ambiguity about what to fix first, or whether to raise the priority of the incident for that screaming customer.

 Concept: timescales

Without a formal process, it's very hard to know how quickly an incident should be fixed, or what to fix first. This causes confusion for IT staff who are trying to manage their workloads, and for customers who need to be able to plan their time.

Timescales need to be agreed for the resolution of incidents with different priority levels. IT can then use this information to break down the incident lifecycle and track how much time should be spent on each stage.

For example, it's good practice to give the Service Desk a fixed amount of time to work on an incident. If they have not been able to resolve a Priority 2 incident in, for example, 30 minutes, they should escalate it to second-line support staff, rather than spending any more time on it.

Timescales can be integrated into the service management tool, which should also allow for automated escalation if a target is going to be breached.

 ## Concept: incident model

Service management recommends the use of models as part of many processes. They are documented, repeatable ways of dealing with repeat occurrences such as incidents, problems and changes. Most organisations see the same incidents over and over again. Documenting what needs to be recorded and what to do means the incident will be handled correctly – whether it's initially recorded by an experienced team member, or a new member of staff.

Incident models will include:

- steps to be taken and their correct order, including any dependencies
- roles and responsibilities
- timescales and targets
- escalation procedures and points

- minimum data set to be captured.

The minimum data set is particularly important if the incident is going to be escalated to second-line support. Many support teams complain they do not get enough information and 'bounce' incidents back to the Service Desk. This wastes time and makes the incident resolution take longer.

Second-line support teams should be invited to provide a list of the minimum data they need to be included in the incident model.

 Concept: major incident

Each organisation needs to define what they mean by a major incident. Major incidents will have a very severe impact on the business (for example, a security breach or loss of a business critical service). They need to be handled in a different way to a normal incident, and will usually be actively managed by a team led by someone in the major incident manager role.

There are two main priorities during a major incident:

1 **Keep all stakeholders informed:** including users, the Service Desk and IT and business management.
2 **Coordinate investigation and recovery activities:** preventing panic and making sure steps are not duplicated or missed.

Once the major incident is complete, a meeting is normally held to review any lessons learned.

Concept: process interfaces

Incident Management needs to develop interfaces across the service lifecycle to be effective.

Service Design interfaces include:

- **Service Level Management:** the targets documented in Service Level Agreements will help with incident prioritisation, and Incident Management can provide an early warning of any potential SLA breaches.
- **Capacity or Availability Management:** incidents may be related to a lack of capacity, or indicate loss of availability. Capacity and Availability Management will provide support during the diagnosis and resolution of this type of incident.
- **Information Security Management:** security-related incidents need to be managed, for example, users trying to install unapproved software. If there are any ways to improve the design of services so that the risk of a breach is reduced, Incident Management will feed these back to Service Design.

Service Transition interfaces include:

- **Service Asset and Configuration Management:** the Configuration Management System is used to aid incident investigation and resolution. The Service Desk and Incident Management can also help configuration management to identify poorly performing configuration items and will often enter updates about CI status changes related to incidents.
- **Change Management:** changes may be needed to resolve incidents. Incidents may be linked to failed changes, or changes that have been implemented, so the

Incident Management process should have access to the change schedule.

Service Operation interfaces include:

- **Problem Management:** this process uses incident records for trend analysis and provides workarounds that support faster incident resolution.
- **Access Management:** incidents may be related to unauthorised access or security breaches. Incident history can be used to support security investigations.

Remember: interfaces could mean Incident Management provides information to a process, or receives information from a process. Every process is more effective when it works with other processes and less effective if it works in isolation.

 Process activities

Figure 35, overleaf, shows the Incident Management process flow.

Notice how service requests are filtered out as early as possible. This helps the Service Desk and support teams to prioritise work correctly, based on the targets associated with the service requests and incidents.

The process flow also shows how functional and hierarchical escalation can be applied to incidents, if required.

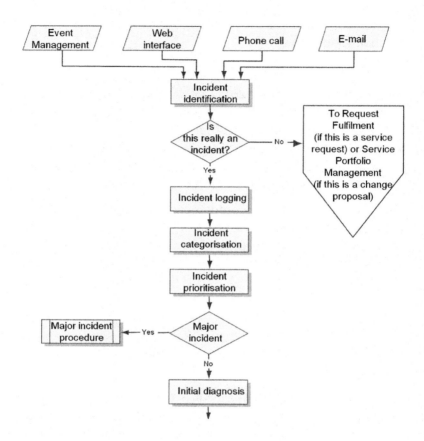

Continued overleaf ...

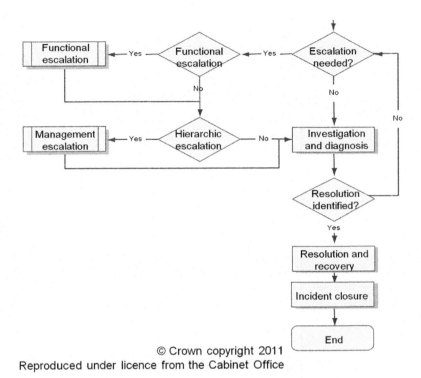

Figure 35: Incident Management process flow

Process step	Explanation
Process trigger	Triggers can be users, monitoring tools, technical staff and other service management processes. Triggers can be received from internal and external sources, for example, an external customer. Triggers can be received by web, monitoring tool, phone call, e-mail or face-to-face visit.

Incident identification	Once the incident has been identified, the Service Desk will raise an incident record. This will be populated with a minimum set of information, including who is raising the incident, date, time and description.
	The record will be updated with more details as the incident progresses.
Is it an incident?	A service request is something that the Service Desk is asked to do that is not triggered by an incident. For example, resetting a password or installing an approved piece of software.
	Service requests will be handled by the Request Fulfilment process, and will have different SLA targets associated with them.
Incident logging	Every single incident must be recorded. These incident records are vital for trend analysis and reporting.
	Some organisations also allow users to log their own incidents via a web front-end or mobile device.
Incident categorisation	Categorisation is a high-level way of splitting up incidents, for example, into hardware and software, or individual services.
	The correct categorisation is really important for assigning the incident to the correct support team and also for producing accurate incident reports.
	Many tools support multi-level categorisation, for example, selecting hardware displays all hardware, which contains printers, selecting printers then displays all the makes and models.

Incident prioritisation	Priority is worked out within Incident Management by looking at two factors – impact and urgency. **Impact** can be calculated by looking at information such as the number of users affected, or the criticality of the service. **Urgency** is a measure of how quickly the business needs the resolution. By multiplying impact and urgency, the incident is given a priority. Prioritising incidents enables support teams to work out which incidents need to be addressed first. **Remember: impact x urgency = priority**
Major incident?	Major incidents have severe levels of impact and urgency and will need to involve additional management resources to ensure they are resolved quickly.
Initial diagnosis	Initial diagnosis normally starts while the user is still on the phone, and this is where the Service Desk will attempt a first time fix. If no first time fix is possible, the incident is passed to the appropriate resolver group.
Functional/ hierarchical escalation	Functional and hierarchical escalation can be invoked at any point.
Investigation and diagnosis	Investigation and diagnosis will be carried out in more depth by the appropriate resolver group(s). If the incident is assigned to the correct group initially, the investigation and diagnosis will happen quickly. Some incidents bounce around between teams which wastes time and can increase the impact to the business.

Resolution and recovery	Resolution and recovery involves the restoration of service to the user. The incident status is typically set to resolved, and returns to the Service Desk for closure.
Incident closure	It is important to note that according to service management principles the only functional area that closes incidents is the Service Desk, with permission from the user affected.
	Second-line support teams will pass the incident back to the Service Desk after resolution, so that they can call the user and confirm the user is happy for the incident to be closed. This final contact makes the incident lifecycle a closed-loop process and ensures that users are satisfied.
	In some organisations, there are not enough resources to contact every user after every incident. In this case, automated e-mails are often used advising the user that their incident will be closed shortly, as the Service Desk believe it is resolved.
	The Service Desk will also take this opportunity to check whether the initial categorisation of the incident was indeed correct. If the categorisation was not correct, it may have been sent to the wrong team initially, losing valuable time during resolution.
	If there are lots of incidents with incorrect categories, this may highlight a training requirement for the Service Desk staff.

Table 20: The Incident Management process

Functional escalation
Functional escalation involves escalating (or passing) the incident from resolver group to resolver group, for example from first-line to second-line and then third-line support. Each area will try to use its skills to resolve the incident and restore service, but pass it on if they are unable to. It's important that one team does not hold an incident for a long time, as this can affect the overall targets for restoring the service.
Hierarchical escalation
Hierarchical escalation involves escalating (or passing) the incident up the management chain, particularly where the incident is a high priority, or where the user is very unhappy. Hierarchical escalation provides additional management support and backing – this is really useful, for example, if we require additional resources, or we need to engage with the next level of technical expertise.

Table 21: Types of incident escalation

 Process considerations

In many organisations, the relationship between the Service Desk and second-line support teams is poor. The Service Desk see second-line support as being arrogant techies who bounce incidents back unnecessarily, won't talk to users and fix things in the order they feel like fixing them.

Second-line support teams see the Service Desk as a nuisance, unqualified staff who send poorly documented incidents that they could have fixed themselves.

Neither of these opinions is completely true.

An effective Incident Management process can help to break down the barriers between the teams. Incident models (contributed to by second-line staff) make sure the right data is recorded and the incident is sent to the right place. Timescales and priorities make sure incidents are fixed in the right order, with no argument about what should be done first.

Incident Management is perfect for automation, and many mature tools exist for this process. When selecting a tool, look for ease-of-use functionality, e.g. integration with phone systems, the ability to auto-populate fields and excellent reporting.

Incident Management can really help to build buy-in for a service management implementation. It can provide fast improvements for end users and brilliant management information for IT as well. If you can start with a process that delivers results quickly, it can be easier to make a case for investment in other service management processes.

One area that trips up a lot of organisations is the level of categorisation they introduce. Keep it simple, and control which roles are allowed to add categories. The category trees in some organisations have had hundreds and hundreds of entries when actually a few dozen would do the job. Be very wary of introducing a 'misc' or 'unknown' category – you might find everything ends up there.

Service Operation process: Problem Management

Many organisations see the same incidents happening repeatedly. They can fix them quickly, but it's much better for everyone if the root cause can be removed, so that the incidents don't actually happen anymore. This is where Problem Management steps in.

 ## *Purpose and objectives*

Problem Management manages the lifecycle of a problem. A problem is defined as *'the unknown cause of one or more incidents'*.

Problem Management will work reactively to try to identify what's causing recurring incidents, and proactively to try to prevent problems before they occur.

Problems are recorded and made available to IT staff, so that other teams can see what progress is being made.

The objectives of Problem Management are to:

- prevent problems and the resulting incidents from happening
- implement cost justified resolutions to eliminate recurring incidents
- minimise the impact of incidents that cannot be prevented.

 ## *Scope*

Problem Management manages problems through their lifecycle. This includes collecting and recording information, managing investigation and diagnosis, and following the Change Management procedure if a corrective change is needed. The process will document known errors that include the root cause of the problem and a workaround that Incident Management can use to temporarily restore service, or reduce the impact of the problem.

Reactive Problem Management works closely with Incident Management to try to identify potential problems from incident records.

Proactive Problem Management will work with processes, such as Availability Management and Capacity Management, to try to identify improvements that might prevent problems from occurring. Other proactive activities include using techniques such as brainstorming and analysis to try to identify where problems will occur.

Problem Management will have a close relationship with CSI, as it investigates the cause of poor service and tries to improve the customer experience.

 Value

Problem Management delivers real, measurable benefits. Incident volumes will be reduced, which in turn reduces the cost of supporting IT services. IT support staff are freed from fixing the same incidents over and over again, so that they can focus on long-term service improvements and more proactive activities.

End users experience fewer incidents so they can also be more productive, getting to use the services that allow them to do their jobs.

An IT department that is fire-fighting all the time will struggle to do any planned work, such as changes or improvements. There is even a risk that key staff will burn out and leave the organisation.

Concept: Incident versus Problem Management

It is important to distinguish between Incident and Problem Management. Incident Management aims to restore service to the business as quickly as possible. This can often mean using temporary fixes – for example, if a PC crashes, then the end user will often be told to reboot it.

Problem Management looks more deeply at the root cause of incidents. For example, if the same PC crashed every day for seven days, Incident Management would keep telling the user to restart their PC. Problem Management might also get involved at this point, to try to work out why that PC kept crashing, and how the issue could be permanently fixed. Perhaps the PC had a virus, or a memory leak that was causing all the incidents. The purpose of Problem Management is to identify and eliminate the underlying root cause of one or more incidents.

 ### Concept: problem analysis techniques

Table 22, overleaf, shows some of the common techniques used during Problem Management activities.

Chronological analysis	This technique produces a timeline of events to reduce confusion about what happened when. It will show what is directly related to the problem, and what events can be discounted.
Pain value analysis	This looks at how much 'pain' the problem is causing the organisation, for example, how many users or services are affected, or what it is costing. This technique is used to support problem prioritisation. Financial Management for IT Services will provide inputs to this calculation.
Kepner and Tregoe	Developed by Charles Kepner and Benjamin Tregoe, this is used to break down and analyse stages of a problem. The stages include: <ul><li>define the problem</li><li>describe the problem (including location, time, etc.)</li><li>establish possible causes</li><li>test probable causes</li><li>verify the true cause.</li></ul>
Brainstorming	A group of stakeholders is gathered together to generate ideas. Each session needs to be carefully facilitated to make sure that everyone participates fully and all ideas are captured.
5 whys	This is a very simple technique. The problem is described, and then a question is posed 'why did this occur?' This question is asked five times, by which time the root cause has probably been arrived at.

Fault isolation	This approach recreates the activities that led to the problem. Each CI involved in the activities is tested, hopefully identifying the CI that caused the failure.
	The approach does not stop when the faulty CI has been found. Every CI is tested to make sure there isn't a second issue that might be missed.
Affinity mapping	Affinity mapping makes sense of large amounts of data by grouping it under headings, based on similar traits.
	It will normally be used during a brainstorming session − where ideas can be written on sticky notes or cards and then moved together. Cards that have been grouped together can then be examined to try to identify a potential root cause.
Hypothesis testing	Technical teams often think they know what's causing a problem, but they aren't always correct. It is good practice to turn their ideas into a series of hypotheses, which can be tested in order − based on the probability of them being correct.
Technical observation post	This approach gathers a group of technical staff to monitor a service or area of infrastructure in real time, normally to try to identify the root cause of an intermittent problem. The benefit comes from gathering the resources together and directing their focus towards the issue.

Ishikawa diagram	This approach produces cause and effect diagrams, and was developed by Kaoru Ishikawa.
	Sometimes known as a 'fishbone' diagram, it uses the problem as the main trunk of the diagram, with possible primary causes branching off it. Possible secondary causes then branch from the primary causes.
	For example, 'e-mail down' might have primary causes of power failure, server down, network down. Power failure might have a secondary cause of 'building work'.
Pareto analysis	The 80/20 rule is familiar to most people. Important causes of failure (for example what generates 80% of incidents) can be highlighted and focused on. More trivial causes are documented and laid aside for future attention.

Table 22: Problem analysis techniques

Different analysis techniques will be used depending on the type of problem and the staff involved.

 Concept: development errors

Although the development teams might not like to admit it, most new services have some errors when they go live.

If problems are detected during development, they should be recorded and the information should be passed to Problem Management as part of the transition and knowledge transfer.

This allows user expectations to be set and stops Problem Management going through the same investigation process again.

 Concept: process interfaces

Problem Management process interfaces include:

- **Financial Management:** helps Problem Management to calculate the pain value of a problem by assessing the cost of the related incidents.
- **Availability and Capacity Management:** these processes support Problem Management when investigating issues related to availability or capacity; and will often share measurements and information.
- **IT Service Continuity Management:** this process may be triggered by an unresolved problem that is having a severe effect on the business.
- **Service Level Management:** this process provides targets and information to support prioritisation; and it also uses information from Problem Management in service reports and reviews.
- **Change Management:** will approve requests for change for any permanent solutions or workarounds, and provide information about the change schedule where a failed change may have caused a problem.
- **Release and Deployment Management:** this process will deploy problem fixes, and may be involved with knowledge transfer to Problem Management relating to development errors.
- **Service Asset and Configuration Management:** provides the Configuration Management System for problem investigation – identifying configuration items

which may be causing problems and helping to get to the root cause.

- **Knowledge Management:** the SKMS can store the Known Error Database and hold or link to problem records.
- **Incident Management:** provides incident records for trend analysis and receives workarounds from Problem Management.
- **Seven-Step Improvement Process:** this process works with Problem Management to rationalise data and identify improvement opportunities.

 Process activities

Figure 36 shows the Problem Management process flow.

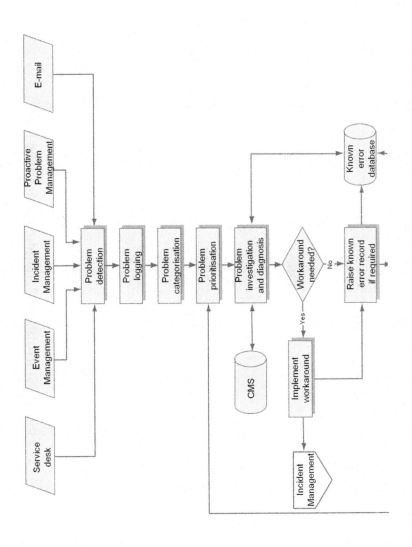

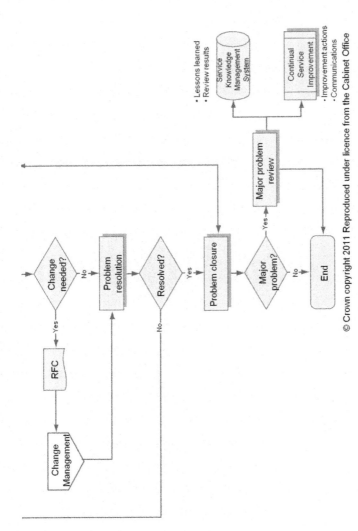

Figure 36: Problem Management process flow

Process step	Explanation
Problem detected	This can come from a number of different sources, including the Service Desk and Incident Management, suppliers, development teams, or trend analysis produced from incident records.
Problem logged	All the relevant details are recorded, including who is affected, when it happened and where it happened. The record will be date and time stamped for reporting purposes. More details will be added as the problem investigation progresses.
Categorisation	Problem categories are likely to be the same as incident categories, for easy cross-referencing.
Prioritisation	The priority is based on impact and urgency, as with incidents. For impact, the number of incidents related to this particular problem will factor into the calculation.
Investigation and diagnosis	Investigation and diagnosis is carried out by the relevant technical teams, with supervision and coordination from the Problem Management process staff. Different analytical techniques are used to try to determine the actual root cause of the problem. Third-party suppliers may be involved at this stage, if appropriate.
Workaround needed?	A workaround is a temporary way of circumventing the problem, so that users can continue working.

	If a workaround is established at this stage, it will be documented and shared with Incident Management who can begin to use this information to support users who are being inconvenienced by the incident.
Create known error record	As soon as the workaround is in place, a known error record is also opened for informational purposes. A known error is typically not opened until a workaround is in place and the root cause has been established, but in theory it can be opened at any time. Known error records imply the organisation is not dealing with an unknown quantity any more – it is dealing with a defined error that can be fixed if cost-justified.
Change needed?	Once the resolution has been found, a request for change will be raised if necessary.
Resolution	The resolution is implemented once approval has been received, and monitored to make sure the problem really is resolved and has been truly eliminated. For some problems, a long period of monitoring is required before the organisation can say the problem is truly fixed.
Closure	The problem is closed with all relevant updates.
Major problem review	A review is held, if needed, to document any lessons learned or ongoing actions.

Table 23: The Problem Management process

Workaround	*'A workaround reduces or eliminates the impact of an incident or problem for which a full resolution isn't yet available.'* For example, restarting a PC might allow a user to carry on working for a short period of time.
	'Workarounds for problems are documented in known error records. Workarounds for incidents that do not have associated problem records are documented in the incident record.'
Known error	A known error is *'a problem that has a documented root cause and a workaround.'*
	A known error is typically raised when the workaround and root cause have been identified. Known errors might be identified by development teams or suppliers, as well as Problem Management.
	Once the root cause of a problem has been identified, the known error record can be created and stored in a repository called the Known Error Database (KEDB).
Known Error Database (KEDB)	The KEDB is *'a database containing all known error records.'* It could be part of the Configuration Management System, or stored in another area of the SKMS.
	The KEDB is a source of information for Service Asset and Configuration Management, as well as the Service Desk/Incident Management who will use it to access workarounds.
	Remember, a known error can be raised whenever it is useful. This might even be before a workaround is complete.

Request for change (RFC)	An RFC might be needed to resolve a problem, or to implement a workaround. Problem Management must follow the appropriate control processes, or it could create more problems.

Table 24: Problem Management outputs

 Process considerations

Problem Management needs to be implemented carefully. If it is set up as a separate team or group, there is a danger it will just become a dumping ground for everything the other support staff find too difficult.

Problem Management should be viewed as a point of coordination for investigation and resolution of problems. Their role is to work with multiple support teams at once, making sure investigation is carried out in a sensible way and actions are documented, so they are not duplicated.

Sometimes an organisation will experience a problem that no one wants to take responsibility for. The network team will insist it's a server issue, and the server team will insist it's an application fault. In this situation, the Problem Management process needs to have the authority to get the teams to work together, eliminating possible causes until the true root cause is left.

Many organisations struggle to differentiate between incidents and problems. It is essential to define and clearly communicate the scope of the two processes. Just because an incident has been open for a long time doesn't make it a problem.

Service management tools can significantly improve the performance and usefulness of Problem Management. If workarounds are easily searchable and problems can be linked to incident records, the process will work well. If it's too hard to find a workaround, the Incident Management staff won't bother and the process won't deliver value.

You don't need to have a mature Incident Management process and lots of incident records to start doing Problem Management. If your incident records are poor, try doing a user and IT staff survey, to find out what they think the top ten recurring incidents are and work from that.

 Service Operation function: the Service Desk

Service Operation is the only one of the ITIL core volumes that goes into detail about specific functions. This isn't to try to dictate how an organisation should be structured – it's to show how critical these support teams are to a successful service provider. Wherever these roles are carried out, they must be aligned to business needs.

We start with the Service Desk – the single point of contact for end users who need support.

 Objectives

The Service Desk is similar to the traditional IT helpdesk, but offers a more complete range of services. The objective of the Service Desk is to restore normal service to users as quickly as possible.

The Service Desk is a single point of contact (SPOC). If a user wants to contact IT, they should always go via the

Service Desk. They should not call or e-mail contacts or colleagues in IT areas such as second-line support.

The Service Desk uses the Incident Management and Request Fulfilment processes. It may also carry out Access Management activities, and update the Configuration Management System under the authority of Service Asset and Configuration Management.

The team leader or manager of the Service Desk is also normally the incident manager, although it is possible the Incident Management process owner could sit elsewhere within an organisation.

The Service Desk meets its goal by using the Incident Management process to restore service as quickly as possible. This could mean providing a temporary fix to a fault using a workaround provided by Problem Management.

The Service Desk keeps ownership of incidents throughout their lifecycle.

Service Desks need to provide excellent levels of customer service, and provide levels of first time fix in line with business requirements.

 Responsibilities

There are a number of areas included as part of a standard Service Desk role:

- **Provide excellent customer service:** The requirements of the business need to be documented and fed into the design of the Service Desk. For example, does the business need a high level of first time fix, or does it just require that incidents are raised promptly and passed to second-line support teams? These requirements will influence the resources needed and the level of skills required on the Service Desk.

- **Provide set levels of accessibility:** The service hours during which the desk will be available need to be agreed, as well as the acceptable ways of contacting the Service Desk. These might include e-mail, phone, fax, instant messaging and via web-based forms for self-service incidents to be raised. Face-to-face visits may be allowed, or not.
- **Provide quick turnaround of incidents and service requests:** The Service Desk provides quick turnaround of requests and incidents using the Incident Management and Request Fulfilment processes. All incidents are owned by the Service Desk through their lifecycle, and the user will get a courtesy call before the incident is closed. Service Desk agents should be well trained and rewarded to maintain high levels of motivation. By working as a team, a skilled set of Service Desk resources will identify incidents and problems, as well as issues that need escalating.
- **Provide reports and management information:** The number of contacts received by the Service Desk is linked to the quality and stability of the services being provided. Incident records can be analysed to identify trends and opportunities for service improvement.

 Service Desk roles

Table 25, overleaf, shows some of the common Service Desk roles and their main responsibilities. Each organisation will structure their Service Desk differently to make sure they meet their customer's needs.

Service Desk manager	This role will be accountable for the Service Desk and will have a number of Service Desk supervisors reporting into it.
	Remember, for every role in the service management organisation, clearly defined job descriptions are needed to make sure each staff member understands their exact role and responsibilities.
	This role is typically responsible for:
	• overall management of desk activities and supervisors
	• acting as a point of escalation
	• taking on a wider customer service role
	• reporting to senior managers on significant or high-impact incidents
	• attending Change Advisory Boards
	• being accountable for incident and service request handling.
Service Desk supervisor	On larger desks or desks offering 24/7 services, this may be fulfilled by more than one individual. On a smaller desk, the role may be fulfilled by the senior Service Desk analyst.
	This role typically includes:
	• managing staffing and shift schedules
	• handling human resources activities
	• acting as an escalation point for difficult calls or incidents, and possibly handling calls during high volume periods
	• producing management reports and statistics, and representing the Service Desk at

	meetings
	• arranging staff training and awareness sessions
	• liaising with senior management and Change Management as needed.
Service Desk analyst	This role mainly consists of providing first-line support, whether by taking calls or answering e-mails and processing data logged in web forms.
	They will be mainly involved in the incident and Request Fulfilment processes. They may also have a role in other service management processes, including Access Management and SACM, but this will be under the control of the process owners.
Super user	Super users may be recruited from the business. They take on some IT responsibilities in addition to their normal business role. Super user responsibilities include:
	• *'facilitation of operational communication between IT and the business*
	• *reinforcing user expectations about agreed service levels*
	• *training for users in their area*
	• *providing support for minor incidents and simple service requests*
	• *being involved with new releases and roll outs'.*
	The super user's line manager must make sure they have time to carry out their additional responsibilities.

Table 25: Service Desk roles

Concept: Service Desk structures

Service Desks can be structured to suit the needs of the organisation and customer base. Typical structure considerations include:

- local
- central
- virtual
- follow the sun
- specialised Service Desk groups.

Centralised Service Desk	Centralised Service Desks are in a single or a small number of locations, and support the whole organisation from there. This can be very resource efficient and cost effective, but some form of local presence may still be required for hardware fixes and desk-side visits.
	Centralised Service Desk staff can develop better skills as they are familiar with frequently occurring incidents for the whole infrastructure.
Local Service Desk	Local Service Desks are located near the users they serve. For example, if an organisation has three offices, there could be a Service Desk in each. Local Service Desks help to build good relationships with the business. They can, however, be less cost efficient than a centralised desk. There is also a risk that individual local working practices can develop – leading to a loss of consistency.
	A local Service Desk may be justified for a number of reasons, e.g. different languages or cultures and time zones. If there are specialised services or users, they may need a local desk to contact, or VIP users may need a local desk.

Virtual Service Desk	Virtual Service Desks use technology and tools to give the impression of a single Service Desk, while using resources located anywhere. For example, all of the Service Desk staff could work from home, but from the user perspective, they still call a single phone number and receive a consistent level of service.
Follow the sun Service Desk	For larger organisations, virtual Service Desks can transform into follow the sun Service Desks. This means that the user will still call a single number, but the organisation is able to take advantage of geographical and global locations to create a follow the sun service. Changing time zones are used to provide 24-hour coverage more cheaply, as people work their shift within their own normal business hours. For a follow the sun Service Desk to work well, the Service Desk analysts all need to have access to the same tool. They also need to adhere to the same processes to work efficiently and provide a consistent service.
Specialised Service Desk groups	Within the Service Desk, groups can be created containing staff with specialised skills. Calls can be routed to different staff allowing incidents to be resolved faster. For example, a routing system might ask callers to 'press 1' for a hardware issue, and '2' for a software issue. Be careful not to make this too complicated though, or it might cause confusion for end users. These groups are usually only implemented for key services, and where financially justified.

Table 26: Service Desk structures

Concept: Service Desk staffing

The Service Desk is the single point of contact for end users getting in touch with the IT service provider. A good Service Desk can reflect well on the whole department, and an ineffective Service Desk can cause real problems for the relationship between IT and its customers. Service Desks need good quality staff. The Service Desk manager needs to be a good team leader and motivator who can remain calm under pressure.

Service Desk analysts need to have the right skills to allow them to manage and resolve incidents in line with business requirements. They will require good customer service skills, business and industry awareness, as well as some technical knowledge.

Service Desks generally have a high turnover of staff due to the pressure of the job. The loss of key team members can have a minimal impact on the team if the necessary processes and procedures are well documented to allow new staff to be trained quickly.

Many organisations struggle to get the right staff for their Service Desk. One common question is 'should I recruit staff with good technical skills, or good customer service skills?'

Technical skills can usually be taught. Customer service skills are much harder to teach. It's easy to refine and improve customer service skills, but if you have someone who doesn't want to help people, it's very hard to change their attitude. Many Service Desk managers look for customer service skills first, knowing that staff with a good attitude will pick up the technical knowledge they need quickly.

Example: Customer service versus technical skills

Concept: super users

In conjunction with the Service Desk, many organisations train and deploy super users. A super user is defined as a user who helps other users, and assists in communication with the Service Desk or other parts of the IT service provider. Super users typically provide support for minor incidents and training to other users.

Super users are given a higher level of training than normal users and can act as a point of liaison between end users and IT. Their role can include cascading information, and providing some initial filtering before a user contacts the Service Desk.

Remember: even if a super user resolves an issue, it must be logged to maintain the incident records.

Super users will typically only act for one application or one business unit, where they have specialised knowledge. Their role can also include training, support during ongoing incidents and service requests, and involvement with releases and rollouts.

The role of the super user must be clearly defined, and their line manager must allow them the necessary time to carry out their role. If not, the position of super user will look very unattractive and business staff are unlikely to volunteer for the role.

 Concept: Service Desk performance measurement

The Service Desk can be a rich source of performance information. The telephone system in use will typically provide metrics such as time to answer or calls abandoned, and the Incident Management tool will show the number of incidents logged, resolved, escalated, and so on.

When measuring Service Desk performance, it is important to concentrate on what's really relevant, not produce pages and pages of reports that serve no real purpose.

A typical Service Desk will use measures including:

- time to answer calls/e-mails
- number of calls abandoned
- length of calls
- number of calls answered by agent
- customer satisfaction survey results
- first-time fix rate
- incidents incorrectly assigned.

These can all be used to assess Service Desk performance at an individual and overall level, and highlight areas for improvement. There will be many other measures related to the Incident Management process too.

Remember: measures need to drive good behaviour. One Service Desk was given a target to improve how quickly they answered calls. Whenever the desk was quiet, the Service Desk agents would call each other – answering instantly and improving their statistics. This did not lead to any measurable improvement for the customer.

 Service Operation function: Technical Management

Technical Management refers to the groups, departments or teams that provide technical expertise and overall management of the IT infrastructure.

Technical Management has a dual role. The first part of the role is to be the custodian of technical knowledge and expertise related to managing the IT infrastructure. As part of this role, Technical Management makes sure the knowledge required to design, test, manage and improve IT services is identified, developed and refined.

The second part of the role is the provision of resources to support the IT service management lifecycle. Technical Management makes sure that resources are effectively trained and deployed to design, build, transition, operate and improve the technology required to deliver and support IT services.

By fulfilling its dual roles, Technical Management makes sure the organisation has access to the right type of human resources that will manage technology to meet business objectives. The requirements for the roles will be defined in strategy and design, validated in Service Transition and refined in Continual Service Improvement.

Technical Management is also responsible for ensuring a balance between skill level, utilisation and cost of resources. If we are paying for expensive technical staff, the level of utilisation needs to deliver return on investment.

 Objectives

The objectives of Technical Management are to help plan, implement and maintain a stable technical infrastructure to support the organisation's business processes.

This is achieved through:

- well designed and highly resilient, cost-effective technical topology

- the use of adequate technical skills to keep the technical infrastructure in optimum condition
- swift use of technical skills to speedily diagnose and resolve any technical failures that do occur.

 Activities

Technical Management activities will include:

- liaising with other process areas, vendors and internal teams
- documenting skills requirements and delivering training related to the infrastructure
- developing documentation related to the infrastructure
- carrying out research and development of new technology that could help the organisation.

 Metrics

Typical metrics used to measure the performance of Technical Management will include:

- measurement of agreed outputs, for example, transaction rates or Service Desk training completed
- process metrics, for example, response time to events or incident resolution times
- technology performance metrics, for example, utilisation rates of memory or processors, or availability of systems
- measurement of maintenance activity, for example, maintenance performed in agreed timescales
- training and skills metrics – do staff have the skills and training required to carry out their role?

Roles

Technical manager/ team leader	Technical managers or team leaders are needed for each team or department. The type and number of roles will depend on the size of the organisation. The role includes: • *'leadership, control and decision making for the team or department* • *providing technical knowledge and leadership for the area covered by the team or department* • *ensuring training, awareness and experience levels are maintained* • *performing line management* • *reporting to senior management on technical issues as required.'*
Technical analysts/ architects	Technical analysts and architects are the resources who carry out all the activities related to Technical Management, except the daily operational tasks that are carried out by technical operators or IT Operations Management. This role includes: • *'working with users, sponsors, Application Management and stakeholders to determine their evolving needs* • *working with Application Management and other technical areas to establish the highest level of system requirements that will meet business needs within budget and technology constraints* • *defining and maintaining knowledge about how systems are related and any dependencies* • *performing cost benefit analyses to determine the most appropriate technology for the business*

	• *developing operational models that will optimize resource utilization and maximize performance* • *configuring the infrastructure to deliver consistent and reliable performance* • *defining all the tasks required to manage the infrastructure.'*
Technical operator	This role refers to any staff members that perform day-to-day operational tasks related to Technical Management. This is normally delegated to IT operations.

Table 27: Technical Management roles

 Service Operation function: Application Management

The Application Management function is performed by any team, department or group that is involved in managing and supporting operational applications.

Application Management also plays an important role in the design, testing and improvement of applications that form part of IT services. Application Management may be involved in development projects, but it's important to remember that this function is not the same as the applications development teams in an organisation.

The role of Application Management is similar to that of Technical Management. Their role, however, applies to applications, not infrastructure.

The scope of Application Management covers both in-house and externally developed applications, and they are often involved in the decision to buy, or build, a particular application.

The high-level roles for Application Management cover the same areas as Technical Management, but with regard to applications – they are responsible for being the custodians of knowledge and provision of resources. The end result should again be a balance between the skill level and utilisation of resources and the cost of each resource.

In addition to their high-level role, Application Management is also responsible for providing guidance to IT operations about how best to carry out ongoing operational management of applications.

 ## *Objectives*

The objectives of Application Management are to support the organisation's business processes by helping to identify functional and manageability requirements for application software. They will then assist in the design and deployment of those applications and the ongoing support and improvement of applications.

The Application Management objectives are fulfilled through:

- applications that are well designed, resilient and cost effective
- ensuring that the required functionality is available to achieve the required business outcome
- the organisation of adequate technical skills to maintain operational applications in optimum condition
- swift use of technical skills to speedily diagnose and resolve any technical failures that do occur.

Concept: buy or build?

Application Management will help an organisation to decide whether to buy applications or develop them internally. The decision is made at management level, but Application Management can provide input including:

- application sizing and workload forecasts
- specification of manageability requirements
- identification of ongoing operational costs
- data access requirements for reporting, or integration into other applications
- investigating to what extent the required functionality can be met by existing tools – and how much customisation will be required to achieve this
- estimating the cost of customisation
- identifying what skills will be required to support the solution
- administration requirements
- security requirements.

These will all help the business to make the right decision about where to source its applications.

 Concept: application development and management

In many organisations, there is an application development team and an application support or management team.

Application development is characterised by:

- activities that end once a solution is created
- a focus on utility and functionality, rather than operation
- usually being applied to internally developed applications

- using a project approach, with staff objectives focused on timescales and project completion
- activities that are simple to budget for
- a focus on the software development lifecycle.

Application Management is characterised by:

- activities that manage the whole application lifecycle
- being applied to internally developed and third-party applications
- a focus on utility and warranty
- the use of repeatable, ongoing processes, rather than a project structure
- staff objectives being related to consistency
- costs being linked to overall IT service delivery costs
- a staff focus on the operation and improvement stages of the software lifecycle.

Recent trends in IT have brought these teams closer together, making developers responsible for support and getting support teams involved in development. This can provide a more responsive service for the business.

For Application Management and development to combine successfully, there needs to be a single point of communication for the business. Staff need to have targets set to reflect both development and operations, and a single Change Management process needs to span both groups.

 Activities

Typical Application Management activities will include:

- identifying and maintaining the knowledge required to manage and operate applications
- initiating training programmes related to applications

- designing and delivering end-user training related to applications
- research and development
- supporting other service management processes, such as Change Management and Availability Management
- collaborating with Technical Management
- managing vendors.

 Metrics

Application Management metrics will include:

- measurement of agreed outputs, for example, whether a user can access an application
- process metrics, such as response time to events and incidents
- measurement of maintenance activity, such as the number of updates applied on time
- measurement of application performance, including response time and availability
- measurement of training and skills development for Application Management staff.

 Roles

Application managers and team leaders	A manager or team leader should be available to each application team or department. The job title and number of roles will vary depending on the size of the organisation.
	The manager or team leader role will include the following responsibilities:
	• 'overall responsibility for leadership, control and decision-making for the applications

	team or department
	• provision of technical knowledge and leadership in the specific applications support activities covered by the team or department
	• ensuring necessary technical training, awareness and experience levels are maintained within the team or department
	• involved with ongoing communication with users and customers regarding application performance and evolving requirements of the business
	• reporting to senior management on all issues relevant to the applications being supported
	• performing line-management for all team or department members'.
Applications analyst/ architect	The applications analyst or architect role is responsible for matching requirements to application specifications. The role will include: • 'working with Technical Management to determine the highest level of system requirements required to meet the requirements within any budget and technology constraints • performing cost–benefit analysis to determine the most appropriate means to meet the stated requirement • developing operational models that will ensure optimal use of resources and the appropriate level of performance • making sure that applications are designed

to be effectively managed • *developing and maintaining standards for application sizing and performance modelling* • *generating a set of acceptance test requirements, together with the designers, test engineers and the user, which determine that all of the high-level requirements have been met, both functional and manageability* • *providing input into the design of configuration data required to manage and track the application effectively'.* Each Application Management team will need an appropriate number of application analysts to perform the day-to-day Application Management activities. Again, the number of roles and the organisation structure chosen will vary from organisation to organisation. Factors such as the size of the organisation and the number, age and complexity of the applications will affect resources required.

Table 28: Application Management roles

 Service Operation function: IT Operations Management

IT Operations Management refers to the department, group or team responsible for carrying out day-to-day operational activities. The IT Operations Management function is defined as being responsible for the ongoing management and maintenance of an organisation's IT infrastructure, to ensure delivery of the agreed level of IT services to the business.

IT Operations Management can also be defined as a set of activities involved in the day-to-day running of the IT infrastructure, to ensure that the agreed levels of service are delivered. It is not necessarily the most glamorous part of IT, but it's essential for maintaining the service delivered to users.

Some of the tasks that are carried out by IT Operations Management will have been defined by Technical Management and Application Management, and then handed over to IT operations to carry out on a regular basis.

IT Operations Management activities break down into two sub-functions:

- **IT operations control** oversees all the operational activities and events, such as console management, job scheduling, back-up and restore, and maintenance activities.

- **Facilities management** refers to the management of physical IT environments including the data centre, including considerations such as power and air conditioning. It also includes management of large-scale operational consolidation projects, such as virtualisation of an organisation's servers. Where (for example) a data centre is outsourced, the scope of facilities management includes management of the contract. The scope of facilities management may also include recovery sites maintained as part of the IT service continuity plan.

The IT Operations Management function also has a dual role. Firstly, it is responsible for executing the activities and performance standards defined during Service Design and tested during Service Transition. The role here can be seen as making any minor adjustments needed to keep the service stable and making any minor improvements identified.

The second part of the role is to add value to the different lines of business. This is fulfilled by IT operations continually reinventing themselves to make sure they stay aligned with and responsive to business requirements, as technology and services evolve.

In order to fulfil its dual role, IT operations staff must have the following attributes:

- they must understand how technology relates to services, and what the relative importance of services is to the business
- they must develop procedures and manuals to support effective working practices
- they must use metrics to show their efficiency, effectiveness and business alignment
- all staff must be trained to a level to allow them to carry out their role
- they must focus both on cost effectiveness and the value of the services that they offer.

 Objectives

IT Operations Management objectives include:

- maintaining the organisational status quo through stable services
- seeking to identify areas for improvements that can deliver improved service at reduced cost

- using operational skills to diagnose and resolve IT failures.

 Metrics

IT Operations Management will be measured to make sure it is efficient and effective. Metrics will focus on process activities, maintenance activities and facilities management activities.

Process activity metrics will include measuring areas such as:

- successful completion of scheduled jobs
- incident resolution and response times
- number of changes implemented and backed out
- number of exceptions to scheduled activities.

Maintenance activities that have been delegated to IT Operations Management will also need to be measured. Metrics here could include:

- maintenance performed to the agreed schedule
- number of maintenance windows exceeded
- maintenance objectives achieved.

The last area of metrics for IT Operations Management relates to facilities management. Some examples here include:

- incidents related to the buildings and their management – for example, carrying out repairs
- number of security events
- power usage statistics and any improvements.

Roles

IT operations manager	The IT operations manager takes overall responsibility for IT Operations Management. This includes overseeing all of IT operations control and facilities management. The role includes: • *'providing leadership, control and decision making* • *taking responsibility for all IT Operations Management teams and departments* • *reporting to senior management about IT operations issues* • *performing line management for IT operations team or department managers and supervisors'.*
Shift leader	Because IT Operations Management often works on a 24/7 basis, there may be a number of shift leaders needed. This role will include: • *'taking overall responsibility for leadership, control and decision-making during the shift period* • *ensuring that all operational activities are satisfactorily performed within agreed timescales and in accordance with company policies and procedures* • *liaising with the other shift leaders to ensure handover, continuity and consistency between the shifts* • *acting as line-manager for all operations analysts on their shift* • *assuming overall health and safety, and security responsibility for the shift if required'.*

IT operations analyst	This role is carried out by senior IT operations staff who will be responsible for making sure that all activities are carried out in the most efficient and effective way. This role may be merged with Technical Management, or it may be carried out by a specialist resource who will have detailed input into areas such as job scheduling.
IT operator	Don't forget, this role is often the same as the technical operator role. This role carries out all the day-to-day activities defined in Technical Management and Application Management. They may also carry out work defined by the IT operations analyst. Typical operator roles include: • *performing back-ups* • *console operations, such as monitoring system status* • *managing print devices and consumables* • *ensuring that batch jobs and archiving are performed* • *running scheduled housekeeping jobs* • *burning images for distribution and installation* • *physical installation of standard equipment in the data centre'.*

Table 29: Operations management roles

Putting Service Operation to work

Service Operation is often the most mature part of the service lifecycle within a service provider or IT organisation. Whilst some service providers find strategy hard to understand and implement, there aren't many people that will argue about the need for a Service Desk, or for Technical Management staff to resolve incidents.

One of the main challenges for Service Operation is the speed of change in both technology and user attitudes. Users expect much more, because they are much more familiar with IT in their home lives, as well as their work lives. Bring your own device (BYOD), mobile working and flexible working all make user support and maintenance of stable services much more challenging.

To get Service Operations working, define two things:

1 Who are your users? For example, if your website is available publicly, is anyone in the world potentially a user?
2 What do you support? For example, if you allow your e-mail service to be accessed via a user's own laptop, where does your support responsibility end?

Service Operation is very visible to end users. It is where value is delivered and improvements will be gratefully received by end users. It can, however, be hard to get investment to maintain and gradually improve services that are live, because the business is reluctant to pay extra for something that's working at the moment.

It is important to make sure that funds are set aside to maintain existing services, as well as to fund the big exciting Service Design projects.

CHAPTER 8: CONTINUAL SERVICE IMPROVEMENT

No IT service is perfect. On the rare occasion a service is fully aligned with business requirements, it won't stay that way for long. Services need to be continually improved to make sure they stay aligned with changing business needs.

Continual improvement can be applied to IT services, its structure and its processes. Service quality, service cost and the efficiency of service delivery all need to be considered as part of any continual improvement initiative.

Continual Service Improvement (CSI) theory

The purpose of the CSI stage of the lifecycle is to make sure services and service management are improved. To do this, CSI must identify where improvements can be made and manage the implementation of improvements.

CSI relies on the ability to measure IT services. If an organisation doesn't understand where it is today, it cannot plan for where it wants to be tomorrow. Organisations must be able to produce management information and service performance metrics to provide tangible evidence of changes to service quality.

CSI has a number of objectives. These may change depending on organisational goals, but will typically include:

- working to improve all stages of the service lifecycle – including CSI itself

- carrying out review and analysis of services, service management processes and service level performance
- identifying improvements to IT services, service management processes and cost effectiveness
- implementing improvements without affecting customer satisfaction
- assessing current measurement methods and identifying any shortcomings
- applying quality management to CSI; many organisations will already have a quality management methodology in place that can be applied to CSI activities, preventing duplication of methodologies.

 Scope

The scope of CSI covers all elements of IT services and service management, including every stage of the service lifecycle. It will focus on the four main areas shown in Table 30, below:

CSI scope	Examples
The health of IT service management	This will include processes, Critical Success Factors and Key Performance Indicators, objectives, goals and whether they are being met.
The alignment of the Service Portfolio with current and future business needs	This will include working with processes such as Business Relationship Management to assess whether the service pipeline and Service Catalogue are populated with the right services to support business goals.

Maturity and capability of people, processes, management structures and organisational structures that support services	The roles and responsibilities in place need to be assessed to make sure they are aligned with the current Service Portfolio; changes to the organisational structure or processes might be required, or training and revised objectives for staff.
Continual improvement of services and service assets	CSI will look at service assets as well as services; changes may be made, for example, to replace poorly performing hardware that is affecting overall service performance – information from Incident and Problem Management will help here.

Table 30: The scope of CSI

To support CSI, organisations will need to carry out maturity assessments, internal and external audits, service reviews and customer satisfaction surveys.

 Value

CSI provides a focal point for improvement. It is much better than having fragmented improvement initiatives happening all over the organisation, leading to duplication and wasted resources.

Introducing a culture of improvement will deliver value. Services will continually improve in both quality and cost effectiveness, and customers can be confident that changes in requirements will be accommodated.

Many organisations spend large amounts of staff time producing reports. With CSI, they can be confident the reports will actually be used, and will lead to tangible results.

CSI concepts

 ### The CSI Register

If you go into an organisation and ask for a list of potential improvements, you're likely to get hundreds – lots more than you can handle or implement at once. CSI needs a way of documenting improvements to make sure that good ideas aren't lost, especially if it's not possible to implement them straight away. To do this, it uses the CSI Register. This can be a piece of paper, a spreadsheet or a complicated system – it doesn't matter as long as things are recorded.

The CSI Register records improvements, and categorises them as small, medium or large undertakings. They also need to be broken down into short-, medium- and long-term initiatives. By comparing the size and timescales for the initiative with the benefits that it will deliver, a prioritised list can be produced.

Priorities need to be regularly reviewed and perhaps automatically raised to make sure that lower priority initiatives do eventually get some attention.

The CSI Register will be held as part of an organisation's SKMS and record information for each potential improvement, including:

- unique identifier
- date raised

- raised by
- size (small/medium/large)
- timescale (short/medium/long)
- description and justification
- priority
- owner
- last review date.

Recording potential improvements and reviewing them regularly makes sure that changing business needs are reflected in the improvements implemented.

The CSI manager is accountable and responsible for producing and maintaining the register – it is very important that it's kept up to date. The register will need to have interfaces to strategic initiatives and other service management processes that will identify improvements. This will include Problem Management, Availability Management, Capacity Management and Service Level Management.

 The CSI approach

To be effective, CSI needs a structured approach. The idea of improvement often creates lots of enthusiasm, but momentum is quickly lost without leadership and structure.

Figure 37, overleaf, shows a possible CSI approach:

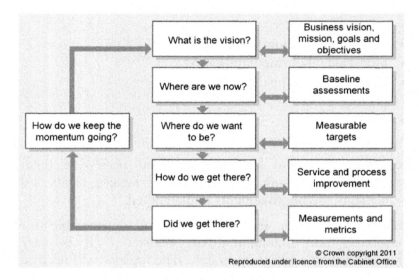

© Crown copyright 2011
Reproduced under licence from the Cabinet Office

Figure 37: CSI approach

The CSI approach is a continual cycle, and has six stages.

CSI approach stage	Considerations
What is the vision?	Without a vision, we have no clear idea where we are going.
	Any vision needs to be aligned with business goals and the overall Service Strategy. The vision defines the aim of the improvement initiative or activity.
Where are we now?	If we don't understand our current position, we cannot plan for our desired future state.
	Every aspect of the organisation – people, processes, suppliers, services and technology – needs to be assessed to give an accurate baseline.

Where do we want to be?	The vision for our improvement might take many years to achieve.
	Without some quick results, there is a risk that the initiative will be seen as a failure. This step allows us to break the vision down into smaller steps, which can be measured and managed.
	The smaller steps still need to be aligned with business requirements.
How do we get there?	CSI needs a plan to deliver the required improvement(s). This will include short-, medium- and long-term activities that will be logged and managed via the CSI Register.
Did we get there?	To be able to say we have been successful, we need to prove it. Agreed measurements and metrics are used to assess whether or not the required changes have been delivered.
How do we keep momentum going?	It can be very challenging to embed change in an organisation. Staff might adopt new ways of working while they are in the limelight, and then quietly go back to older ways of doing things.
	Keeping momentum going makes sure that changes do not slip backwards, and continually seeks new opportunities for improvement.

Table 31: The CSI approach

Measurement and metrics

CSI relies on measurement and metrics. Without solid evidence showing where services are under-performing, CSI will not be able to identify and prioritise improvements. Metrics are scales of measurement. They define what will be measured and provide a quantitative assessment.

There are three main types of metric that support CSI: service, process and technology.

- **Service metrics** measure end-to-end service performance. They will often be built using technology and process metrics. Customers will usually find service metrics easy to understand and feel that they reflect their experience. They might, for example, show service availability during agreed service hours.

- **Process metrics** measure how well a service management process is performing. They will include Critical Success Factors, Key Performance Indicators and activity metrics, for example, the Incident Management process might be measured on the number of incidents with missing information.

- **Technology metrics** *'are often associated with component and application-based metrics such as performance, availability, etc.'* These metrics are normally used within IT and are not as appropriate for customers. They could measure, for example, server performance or CPU utilisation.

CSI will also assess the Critical Success Factors (CSFs) and Key Performance Indicators (KPIs) in use within an organisation.

Remember, a CSF is *'something that must happen if an IT service, process, plan, project or other activity is to succeed. Key Performance Indicators are used to measure the achievement of each Critical Success Factor.'*

A KPI is *'a metric that is used to help manage an IT service, process, plan, project or other activity. Key Performance Indicators are used to measure the achievement of Critical Success Factors. Many metrics may be measured, but only the most important of these are defined as Key Performance Indicators and used to actively manage and report on the process, IT service or activity. They should be selected to ensure that efficiency, effectiveness and cost effectiveness are all managed.'*

Immature service management organisations often try to implement far too many CSFs, with far too many supporting KPIs. This only serves to confuse the audience, rather than making things clearer. CSI will make sure that the CSFs and KPIs in place are the right ones. Any redundant or duplicate measures can be removed.

The KPIs in use within an organisation need to be quantitative and qualitative. This means they need to measure tangible facts (for example, the number of incidents) and intangible emotional responses (for example, customer satisfaction with the Service Desk), respectively.

Every KPI in place should have a purpose. It needs to be easily understood, and should have an owner to make sure it is measured, reported and analysed. As part of the measurement it carries out, CSI will produce baselines. These show what the organisation looks like at a particular point in time, so that comparisons can be made later. This is a similar idea to the configuration baseline we reviewed as part of the Service Asset and Configuration Management process – it's a point for later comparison.

If a baseline hasn't been documented and agreed, it can be very hard to prove that improvements have been made. If no data or previous baselines exist, the first measurements taken are the first baseline. A mature organisation will produce baselines at different levels: strategic, tactical and operational.

 ## *The Deming Cycle*

The Deming Cycle (also known as the Deming circle or Plan-Do-Check-Act cycle) is an important model for CSI. The cycle has four main stages:

- **Plan**: create a plan of activities, including roles and responsibilities.
- **Do**: implement the plan.
- **Check**: assess whether the plan delivered what it was supposed to.
- **Act**: carry out any corrections or new actions required.

The Deming Cycle is used during the implementation of CSI, and during the implementation of improvements. It is based on incremental improvements, not huge changes that the organisation may struggle to cope with.

When CSI is being implemented, the whole cycle is used to make sure that CSI will deliver the required results. Once CSI is established and making improvements to services and service management, the focus moves to the check and act stages. Services and processes are monitored to assess if they are effective, and corrected if they are not.

The Deming Cycle is used in many quality standards. For example, ISO/IEC 20000 (the standard for service management) recommends this approach. The cycle is shown in Figure 38, below.

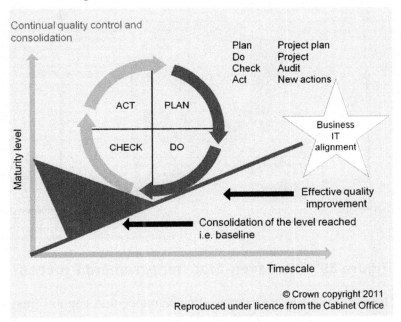

© Crown copyright 2011
Reproduced under licence from the Cabinet Office

Figure 38: The Deming Cycle

CSI process: the Seven-Step Improvement Process

Figure 39, overleaf, shows the Seven-Step Improvement Process, which can be mapped onto the Deming Cycle.

The process can be used to add more depth to each step of the Deming Cycle, leading on to justified improvements in service quality and cost effectiveness.

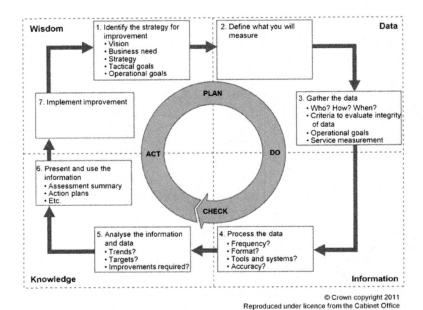

Figure 39: The Seven-Step Improvement Process

The process addresses service performance and capabilities, processes, partners and technology involved with service delivery. It can be applied to the full service lifecycle, not just to live services.

 Purpose and objectives

The purpose of the Seven-Step Improvement Process is to define and manage the steps needed to identify, define, gather, process, analyse, present and implement improvements.

All improvements need to be cost justified. If an improvement cannot be cost justified, it should not be implemented. Improvements need a business case or some form of financial justification.

The objectives of the Seven-Step Improvement Process include:

- to identify improvements
- to reduce the cost of service provision and make sure services meet business requirements
- to identify measurements needed to justify improvement
- to continually review services and service achievement
- to understand what to measure and why.

 Scope

The scope of the Seven-Step Improvement Process includes services, processes, partners and technology right across the lifecycle. Improvements make sure that services stay aligned to changing business needs, and remain attractive to customers.

Remember, CSI is not exempt from improvement and may even improve itself.

CSI also applies to people. Changes in structure or a training initiative could deliver improvements quickly, leading to better service for customers. If staff are over-worked, or don't have the skills to do their jobs, morale will suffer and staff turnover will increase. This can decrease the quality of service provision and increase costs.

The scope includes analysis of the performance and capabilities of services, processes, partners and technology across the lifecycle. Technology use is optimised, and services can be aligned with business needs.

 Value

The Seven-Step Improvement Process provides a structure to measure IT service delivery and assess how well it is performing. This makes sure that IT services and service management are continually improved and aligned with business requirements.

 Process activities

Table 32, below, shows the steps in the process in detail:

Process step	Considerations
Identify the strategy for improvement	The vision for improvement needs to be defined and linked to business goals. This can then filter down through the organisation to feed into tactical and operational goals.
	Without clear direction, there is a real risk that the improvement process will flounder.
Define what you will measure	Services, processes and technology all need to be measured. At this point, an organisation might identify that it doesn't have the right tools to carry out the measurement. This may need to be rectified before the process can move on.
	Step two should be iterative through the rest of the process, but is ignored in many organisations because IT thinks 'they already know what needs to be done'.

Gather the data	Monitoring activities collect data on services, processes, technology and suppliers. Monitoring requirements and settings may need to change over time as the organisation matures, or services evolve. Organisations need to define clearly what data they wish to gather and where it will come from.
Process the data	Data processing takes raw data and adapts it to suit the requirements of the audience. The staff receiving the data need to be able to understand the message being delivered. Data from different sources needs to be normalised, so that an 'apples to apples' comparison can occur.
Analyse the information and data	Analysis takes information and assesses it in the context of what is happening in the organisation. For example, information about hardware failure, number of calls to the Service Desk and falling customer satisfaction can all be linked to the same cause. Analysis is where improvements are identified. It's very important not to jump to conclusions earlier in the process.
Present and use the information	Information is presented to the audience who will be making decisions about improvements. They need to receive the right information at the right time, and in the right format. The audience may be customers, senior management, internal IT teams or suppliers. They will all need different information to make the correct decision.

Implement improvement	Improvements are implemented once the need is understood. Improvements should be cost justified and aligned to business needs.
	This step of the process will then feed back into the vision, and the process begins again.

Table 32: The Seven-Step Improvement Process

For the Seven-Step Improvement Process to be effective, it needs information from other service management processes: Service Level Management, Availability and Capacity Management, Event Management, Incident Management, Financial Management and Change Management will all be closely involved.

The interfaces between processes need to be understood and carefully mapped to make sure the correct information is delivered when required.

 Process considerations

What needs to be fixed or improved in an organisation can be a very subjective matter. Everyone will have a different opinion about what is wrong and what needs to be fixed first, based on the services they use and their own experience and world view.

Service providers are as guilty as customers and users in this area. They make assumptions about what needs to be fixed and what's important to the business, without having all the information they need.

Following a process like the Seven-Step Improvement Process provides structure for improvement activity. The first time you follow the process, it will feel laborious, manual and difficult, but it should get you to the result you need. The next time you follow the process, it will be a bit easier, and it will get easier and easier as the iterations repeat.

There is no feeling worse than standing in front of senior management presenting something based on inaccurate or incomplete data. Use the process to make sure your data stacks up, and test your findings on your peers before you take them to the management team.

Putting CSI to work

To make CSI work in your organisation, here are some important points to consider.

CSI is about cultural change: the primary mistake made when implementing CSI is to allocate staff to roles and think 'job done'. CSI needs to run through every activity and every role in the organisation. If CSI is seen as a team, the team will quickly become a dumping ground for everything hard and problematic.

CSI does not just apply to live services: improvements made early in the lifecycle can be much more effective. For example, it is widely accepted that making corrections to a service during design is much more cost effective than fixing a service that has gone live.

Don't jump to conclusions: many organisations start by implementing improvements. They don't carefully assess what is wrong, or what needs to be done, because they assume that they already know. This is dangerous and can lead to resources being wasted and IT appearing arrogant.

Effective CSI relies on a balanced set of measurements: service providers need to measure the emotional, intangible indicators (for example, customers who 'just aren't happy') and the tangible facts (for example, 'time to complete a transaction'). Both areas are required to get a holistic view of overall service performance.

Don't get carried away with the measurements: modern technology allows us to measure every element of a service, producing far more data that we are equipped to handle. Focus on a few, meaningful measurements and expand from there, if you need to. The more mature the service management organisation, the less they tend to measure.

CHAPTER 9: SERVICE MANAGEMENT AUTOMATION

The benefits of automation

Once a task or process has been introduced and performed regularly, the next step is often to try to automate it. Automation can improve the performance of people, processes, management and organisation structures. It can also improve the way that knowledge and information is shared between parts of the organisation.

Automation can improve the utility and the warranty of services. Some of the areas of improvement include:

- automated resources can have their capacity adjusted easily
- automated resources don't need human intervention, so can be available across time zones or service hours
- automated systems can be measured and improved
- computers can optimise services and processes in ways that humans could not
- automation can capture knowledge about a process, and share it more easily.

Used carefully, automation can improve service quality and reduce costs and risks. It does this by removing the human element and minimising the chances of a task being performed in different ways by different people.

Automation should reduce complexity and uncertainty. To be automated, a task or process must be clearly defined and understood, or the automation will fail.

Areas of service management that will benefit from automation include:

- '*design and modelling*
- *the Service Catalogue*
- *pattern recognition and analysis*
- *classification, prioritisation and routing – for example, during Incident Management*
- *detection and monitoring*
- *optimisation*'.

 Getting ready to automate

Automation will only work if the task or process is broken down into logical steps as part of a workflow that can be programmed into the relevant tool.

There are four main areas to consider when looking at automation:

Automation consideration	Details
Simplify the process before automating	Simplification on its own can reduce variation, and should not adversely affect the process outcome. However, removal of necessary information or tasks will make the process less useful.
	As a general rule, simplify as far as possible without negative effect, and then automate from this point.

Clarify the process before automation	This will include process activities, tasks and interaction, and inputs. Automate, clarify, test, modify and then automate again, being sure to involve all process agents and stakeholders.
Reduce end user contact with the underlying systems and processes	We need to try to present our customers with simple options, so that they can easily present demand and extract utility. For example, if a user is requesting a work station for a new starter, that's what they want to do. They should not have to answer an endless list of questions about what type of PC they want, how much memory, which supplier it will be ordered from, and so on.
Don't rush to automate complex or non routine tasks	Automation is of benefit to high volume, low complexity processes. Not everything is suitable for automation, and we may have to accept that some processes are too complex, or not mature enough, to be automated.

Table 33: Preparing for automation

 Service management automation

Most service management processes will benefit from automation. For example, Incident Management works well when incident information can be captured and easily transferred between teams. Incident Management tools can also automatically notify someone when they are about to breach a target and need to be escalated.

There are many service management tools available now, aimed at small, medium and large organisations. Selecting the correct tool can be a real challenge.

When selecting a tool, remember these key points:

- invest time in requirements gathering, including analysis of your existing toolset: it will pay off
- create a long list of available options
- carry out a paper review
- create a short list and invite suppliers in to demonstrate
- select the tool most closely aligned with your budget and requirements.

Every organisation will have different requirements for a service management toolset, but there are some generic considerations, as shown in Table 34, below.

Generic toolset requirement	Considerations
Self-help	Self-help allows users to access a range of services without speaking directly to someone in the IT department. It is often offered via a web front-end, which needs to connect directly to back-end process handling software.
	Self-help technology integrates these user requests into the back-end process management software, so that they can be treated in a consistent manner.
	Using technology and automation in this way can mean, for example, that fewer people are required on the Service Desk answering the phone, and phone calls could be limited to service emergencies and high priority incidents.

Workflow/ process engine	Automation of workflows and process flows helps ensure that less manual intervention is required when information is passed from team to team, or person to person.
	Responsibilities, mandatory activities and escalation points can also be programmed into a tool with workflow management – so that these are automatically managed too.
Integrated CMS	An integrated CMS allows information about specific configuration items to be accessed at any time. Configuration items can be linked to incidents, problems, changes and known errors – all via the integrated CMS.
Discovery/ deployment/ licensing	Automated discovery tools dramatically ease the task of updating and changing data in a CMS. By automatically discovering every configuration item on the network, only non-networked configuration items will need to be manually discovered and recorded. This removes the danger of people making mistakes during the population of the CMS, and allows ongoing verification of the data.
	Any unauthorised changes made to a configuration item will be quickly picked up by the discovery software. This means you can prevent unauthorised items being connected to the network, as well as identifying any configuration items that disappear without approval.
	Discovery technology can also be used to deploy software packages. This helps the organisation to keep track of their software licensing position, as software installs can quickly be compared to the number of licenses entered in the CMS.

	An interface to self-help facilities can also be provided via the toolset, to allow request and download of approved software. If this is automatically handled by the deployment software, the service request can be fulfilled with no human intervention, again saving resources.
Remote control	Remote control allows an agent to operate an end user's PC from another location.
	With remote control, the Service Desk can resolve more incidents at the first point of user contact. Remote control facilities involve security implications and these will need to be considered carefully. The organisation might, for example, require a user to click to accept an agent having access to their PC.
Diagnostic utilities	Diagnostic utilities include specially written scripts, routines and programs that are executed in order to analyse information quickly and provide feedback, typically to help diagnose or record an incident.
	Within many support organisations, second-line support teams are often critical of the quality of information passed to them by the Service Desk. By involving these teams in the preparation of diagnostic utilities and scripts, the Incident Management process can be made more efficient by ensuring that the correct level of information is collected first time.
	Utilities and scripts will also need to be regularly audited to make sure they are still up to date and fit-for-purpose.

Reporting	All service management tools should come with some pre-programmed reports that you can quickly leverage, as well as offering the option to create your own reports – these should be tailored to your organisation and the specific targets you have to meet. Effective reporting is vital to service management, so any data entered into a toolset should be easy to manipulate and review.
Dashboards	Dashboards provide instant information about service management. For example, a dashboard can allow SLA target breaches to be quickly identified and appropriate action taken. Many organisations already use dashboards, often with red-amber-green colours signifying certain conditions. Dashboards can be used within IT, or made available to customers as well.

Table 34: Generic service management toolset requirements

CHAPTER 10: SERVICE MANAGEMENT TRAINING AND QUALIFICATIONS

Service management can only be successful if staff have the right skills to do their job. Staff who don't have the right skills may feel de-motivated, and won't understand how their role contributes to the value that the customer receives. As services change and evolve, staff may need training or different roles to evolve with them.

The whole service lifecycle depends on trained, motivated and experienced staff. Staff need to understand business priorities, and how IT supports them. They need customer service skills, and the ability to innovate. Staff need to be willing to follow and improve processes and procedures.

Many ITIL roles share generic requirements. These include:

- management skills
- meeting-management skills
- communication skills – both written and verbal
- negotiation skills
- an analytical mind.

Service management staff and skill sets can be managed more easily, if standard roles and job titles are used. Many organisations are adopting frameworks such as the Skills Framework for the Information Age, to help assign skills to roles. You can read more about the skills framework at *www.sfia.org.uk*.

From a service management perspective, training helps a service provider to improve its capabilities. Approved ITIL training, via the official qualification scheme, is a quality controlled way for service provider organisations to develop their staff. This will deliver personal benefits and organisational benefits.

 The ITIL qualification scheme

The ITIL qualification scheme has four levels:

- Foundation
- Intermediate
- Expert
- Master.

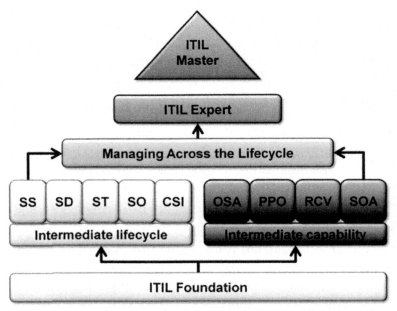

© APM Group – The Accreditor Ltd 2011

Figure 40: The ITIL qualification scheme

Successfully passing the Foundation exam is mandatory before you can progress to other courses, and counts as two credits.

Once you have completed the Foundation exam, you can start to take Intermediate qualifications and, if you wish, work towards your advanced ITIL qualification, known as the ITIL Expert. Getting the ITIL Expert qualification relies on you accruing further credits by choosing courses from the lifecycle and capability streams. You can focus exclusively on one stream, or choose courses from both.

Lifecycle courses are aimed towards delegates who will implement and manage ITIL processes. They take a management perspective of an individual lifecycle phase, such as Service Design or Service Strategy. These courses do not go into detail about the individual process activities.

Capability courses are aimed towards delegates who will be executing ITIL processes on a day-to-day basis. These courses have much more focus on the activities within each process.

After you have accrued enough credits from the lifecycle and capability layer, you will need to do a final, capstone course called Managing across the Lifecycle.

Once you have completed the mandatory Managing across the Lifecycle exam and accrued a minimum of 22 credits, you will then automatically be awarded Expert status, without having to take any further exams.

There is also an advanced service management qualification known as the ITIL Master. This qualification involves preparing a detailed overview of your work in service management across the service lifecycle. This will be reviewed by a panel of industry experts, who will invite you to an interview to discuss your overview.

Master is aimed towards ITIL Experts who also have ITIL implementation experience. It requires candidates to use their experience to explain how they have selected and applied service management principles, techniques methods and knowledge to achieve desired outcomes.

You can read more about all the ITIL qualifications at the official site (*www.itil-officialsite.com*).

CHAPTER 11: MULTIPLE CHOICE EXAM STRATEGIES

This chapter contains some guidance for those using this book to prepare for the ITIL Foundation Certificate in IT Service Management.

Once you have successfully passed your exam, you can use this book as a reference guide and you may not need to look at this chapter again.

The ITIL Foundation Certificate in IT Service Management

The Foundation certificate provides formal certification that a delegate has a good general understanding of ITIL concepts and processes. It is a compulsory, entry-level certificate before delegates can take any higher-level ITIL exams. This book provides you with all the information you need to successfully take the ITIL Foundation exam, as well as lots of extra information not covered in the syllabus.

If you're preparing for the exam, you should download a copy of the latest syllabus from the ITIL official site: *www.itil-officialsite.com/*. You can use it to help direct your studies.

Sample exams

As part of your preparation, you should do as many sample exam questions as possible. You can download a free sample exam paper from the ITIL official site. Other questions are available on the Internet, but remember these may not be official, current or quality controlled.

Sample exams help you to:

- understand the question format and the language used
- test your time management strategies
- gauge your readiness for the real thing.

We're going to discuss some strategies for multiple choice exams and break down some sample questions.

The ITIL Foundation exam has 40 questions and lasts for one hour. You need to get 26 correct to pass – the pass percentage is 65%. The exam is closed book, and there is no negative marking, or trick questions.

Approaching multiple choice exams

Here are some general points to remember when you sit any exam:

- **Read the question carefully:** if you're not careful, you will answer the question you think you see, not the one that's actually on the paper. We're all trained to speed read these days – try dragging your finger along the question, so you don't miss a vital word (like 'NOT').
- **Don't panic!** if your mind goes blank, move on and look at something else. Your subconscious mind will work away even when you're answering a different question.
- **Use the process of elimination:** each question has four possible answers – if you can discount one or two of them, then you've dramatically increased your odds of picking the right answer.
- **Trust your instinct:** one of the most common bits of exam feedback I've heard is delegates who wish they

hadn't changed their answer. It's fine to check over what you've done, but be very wary if you're changing things.

- **Manage your time:** you have one-and-a-half minutes per question. I've never yet had a delegate tell me they ran out of time on the Foundation exam, but some have come close! Don't spend too long staring at one question, when there are easy marks to be picked up further on in the paper.

- **Practice the 'four sweep' approach:** on your first sweep through the exam paper, pick off the easy questions. If you've answered 23 questions easily, that takes the pressure off for your second sweep. Sweep two: spend more time on the challenging questions, but leave anything you really don't know for sweep three. Calculate how many answers you're confident of again. Sweep three: pick off those tough questions. Finally, sweep four: the sense check. Be wary of changing your answers, but look out for that question where you knew the answer was D and you've written C by mistake.

Multiple choice exam question analysis

Let's take a look at a few examples of multiple choice exam questions. These are not questions from an official Foundation exam, or sample exam, but they are a similar level of difficulty.

1   Which of these options is NOT one of the three service classifications?

   a) Core
   b) Enabling
   c) Internal
   d) Enhancing

The first thing to pay close attention to here is the word NOT. Even if it's in bold and capital letters, it's easy to miss. Read the question carefully and focus. This question can also be tough because all the options seem like plausible, ITIL words. It is really important as part of your exam preparation to study, study, study the definitions and key concepts. Use spider diagrams, lists, mnemonics, flash cards – whatever works for you.

The correct answer is c).

2   Which stakeholder will normally buy goods or services, and define what they want the service to do?

a) Customer
b) User
c) Supplier
d) Service provider

This is one of those questions where we can eliminate some options. We can look at the options and rule out the supplier or the service provider, because they don't tell the customer what they want. So, we're choosing from two options instead of four.

The correct answer is a).

3   Which of these is an example of a function?

a) Service Desk
b) Service Owner
c) Process Owner
d) Process Manager

One of these things is not like the others. Analyse the options carefully and what you have is three roles and one function. Again, they are all correct pieces of ITIL terminology, but the three incorrect answers are linked and the correct answer stands alone.

The correct answer is a).

4 Which of these is not one of the four process characteristics?

a) Responds to triggers
b) Delivers a specific result
c) Delivers value to a customer or stakeholder
d) Is timely

This is another example of a question directly linked to the Foundation syllabus. If you learn the four process characteristics, you'll be fine. Be wary of terminology that looks like good service management, but doesn't actually mean anything or doesn't apply to the question.

The correct answer is d).

5 Which of the following processes is NOT described in detail in the *Service Design* core volume?

a) Availability Management
b) Service Level Management
c) Capacity Management
d) Service Portfolio Management

This type of question throws many delegates because it is quite simple. They look at it, panic, and their brain freezes. If you need time to think about a question, come back to it later. You might already half know the answer, and there might be another piece of information in a later question that confirms what you are thinking.

The correct answer is d).

CHAPTER 12: FURTHER READING/RESOURCES

These links will provide further information on some of the topics covered in this book.

General information

ITIL Glossary of Terms: *www.itil-officialsite.com/InternationalActivities/TranslatedGlossaries.aspx*

Mintzberg, the four Ps of strategy: *www.ifm.eng.cam.ac.uk/research/dstools/mintzbergs-5-ps-for-strategy/*

Kepner Tregoe Problem Management technique: *www.kepner-tregoe.com/*

Skills Framework for the Information Age (SFIA): *www.sfia.org.uk*

IT Service Management Forum: *www.itsmfi.org*

Val IT™ for Business Technology Management: *www.isaca.org/Knowledge-Center/Val-IT-IT-Value-Delivery-/Pages/Val-IT1.aspx*

COBIT®: *www.isaca.org/Knowledge-Center/cobit/Pages/Overview.aspx*

CMMI: *http://cmmiinstitute.com/*

Risk management

The Institute of Risk Management: *www.theirm.org*

Management of Risk (M_o_R®): *www.mor-officialsite.com/*

ITIL education

List of ITIL Examination Institutes: *www.itil-officialsite.com/ExaminationInstitutes/ExamInstitutes.aspx*

List of ITIL Accredited Training Organisations: *www.itil-officialsite.com/TrainingOrganisations/ATOListing.aspx*

ITG RESOURCES

IT Governance Ltd. sources, creates and delivers products and services to meet the real-world, evolving IT governance needs of today's organisations, directors, managers and practitioners. The ITG website (*www.itgovernance.co.uk*) is the international one-stop-shop for corporate and IT governance information, advice, guidance, books, tools, training and consultancy.

www.itgovernance.co.uk/itil.aspx is the information page on our website for ITIL resources.

Other Websites

Books and tools published by IT Governance Publishing (ITGP) are available from all business booksellers and are also immediately available from the following websites:

www.itgovernance.eu is our euro-denominated website which ships from Benelux and has a growing range of books in European languages other than English.

www.itgovernanceusa.com is a US dollar-based website that delivers the full range of IT Governance products to North America, and ships from within the continental US.

www.itgovernanceasia.com provides a selected range of ITGP products specifically for customers in the Indian sub-continent.

www.itgovernance.asia delivers the full range of ITGP publications, serving countries across Asia Pacific. Shipping from Hong Kong, US dollars, Singapore dollars, Hong Kong dollars, New Zealand dollars and Thai baht are all accepted through the website.

www.27001.com is the IT Governance Ltd. website that deals specifically with information security management, and ships from within the continental US.

Toolkits

ITG's unique range of toolkits includes the IT Governance Framework Toolkit, which contains all the tools and guidance that you will need in order to develop and implement an appropriate IT governance framework for your organisation. For a free paper on how to use the proprietary Calder-Moir IT Governance Framework, and for a free trial version of the toolkit, see *www.itgovernance.co.uk/calder_moir.aspx*.

There is also a wide range of toolkits to simplify implementation of management systems, such as an ISO/IEC 27001 ISMS or an ISO/IEC 22301 BCMS, and these can all be viewed and purchased online at *www.itgovernance.co.uk*.

Training Services

IT Governance offers an extensive portfolio of training courses designed to educate information security, IT governance, risk management and compliance professionals. Our classroom and online training programmes will help you develop the skills required to deliver best practice and compliance to your organisation. They will also enhance your career by providing you with industry-standard certifications and increased peer recognition. Our range of courses offers a structured learning path from foundation to advanced level in the key topics of information security, IT governance, business continuity and service management.

ISO/IEC 20000 is the first international standard for IT service management and has been developed to reflect the best practice guidance contained within the ITIL framework. Our

ITG Resources

ISO20000 Foundation and Practitioner training courses are designed to provide delegates with a comprehensive introduction and guide to the implementation of an ISO20000 management system and an industry-recognised qualification awarded by APMG International.

Full details of all IT Governance training courses can be found at *www.itgovernance.co.uk/training.aspx*.

Professional Services and Consultancy

As IT service management becomes ever more important in organisations, so the deployment of best practice (e.g. ITIL), or the development of a management system that can be certified to ISO/IEC 20000, becomes a greater challenge; especially when the management systems have to be integrated to achieve the most cost-effective and efficient corporate structure.

IT Governance has substantial real-world experience as a professional services company specialising in IT GRC-related management systems. Our consulting team can help you to design and deploy IT service management structures, such as ITIL and ISO20000, and integrate them with other systems, such as ISO/IEC 27001, ISO22301, ISO14001 and COBIT®. Like ITIL itself, we pride ourselves in being vendor neutral and non-prescriptive in our mentoring approach, transferring the knowledge that you need to document, challenge and improve.

For more information about IT Governance consultancy for IT service management, see *www.itgovernance.co.uk/itsm-itil-iso20000-consultancy.aspx*.

365

Publishing Services

IT Governance Publishing (ITGP) is the world's leading IT-GRC publishing imprint that is wholly owned by IT Governance Ltd.

With books and tools covering all IT governance, risk and compliance frameworks, we are the publisher of choice for authors and distributors alike, producing unique and practical publications of the highest quality, in the latest formats available, which readers will find invaluable.

www.itgovernancepublishing.co.uk is the website dedicated to ITGP, enabling both current and future authors, distributors, readers and other interested parties to have easier access to more information, allowing them to keep up to date with the latest publications and news from ITGP.

Newsletter

IT governance is one of the hottest topics in business today, not least because it is also the fastest moving.

You can stay up to date with the latest developments across the whole spectrum of IT governance subject matter, including risk management, information security, ITIL and IT service management, project governance, compliance and so much more, by subscribing to ITG's core publications and topic alert e-mails. Simply visit our subscription centre and select your preferences: *www.itgovernance.co.uk/newsletter.aspx*.

CPSIA information can be obtained
at www.ICGtesting.com
Printed in the USA
BVOW11s2108080616

451208BV00008B/107/P